AMRITABINDU

AND

KAIVALYA UPANISHADS

A. MAHADEVA SASTRI

GYAN

Published by

GYAN

Gyan Publishing House
5, Ansari Road
Daryaganj, New Delhi-110002
Phone: 011-47034999, 9811692060
E-mail: books@gyanbooks.com

Distribution Network
gyanbooks.com
India, USA, Canada, UK, Australia

ISBN: 978-93-7014-685-3 (HB)

First Published, 1898

2nd Impression 2025

Printed at: Gyan Press, Delhi.

AMRITABINDU AND KAIVALYA UPANISHADS
Author: A. MAHADEVA SASTRI

VEDIC RELIGION.

MINOR UPANISHADS VOL. I.

AMRITABINDU

AND

KAIVALYA UPANISHADS

WITH COMMENTARIES

TRANSLATED INTO ENGLISH

BY

A. MAHADEVA SASTRI, B. A.,

Curator, Government Oriental Library, Mysore.

Madras:

PRINTED BY THOMPSON AND CO., AT "MINERVA" PRESS,

POPHAM'S BROADWAY.

1898.

CONTENTS.

PAGES.

INTRODUCTION.

The mind has been a great bugbear to all philosophers. In seeking to find out what things are in themselves as distinguished from what they appear to be, the ontologist, like any other enquirer, must ultimately resort to the mind for data on which to base his speculations. But all knowledge acquired through the mind comes invested with the limitations under which it works. Everything that is known is tinged with the colour of the mind perceiving it. The metaphysician, therefore, who suspects that things are not what they appear to be, concludes that things in themselves,—the noumena underlying the phenomena,—are inconceivable and unknowable, though he is instinctively led to believe in them. As opposed to him there is a metaphysician of another school, who holds that what is known or conceivable can alone be said to exist, and that therefore whatever is unknown and unknowable and even inconceivable can never be said or thought to exist.

A third position is also possible. It may be that the mind as it is at present constituted is biassed and subject to limitations. If, however, it be possible to divest the mind of all its limitations and imperfections, to make it quite colourless and unbiassed, it will also be possible to know what things are in themselves. The establishment of the validity of this position is the unique pride of the Brahmavâdin. He has from time immemorial proclaimed the possibility of knowing the Thing in itself, and he has had distinguished representatives in the historical period, such as S'rí-Gaudapâdâchârya and his pupil's pupil S'rî-S'ankarâchârya, not to mention a host of others in the later periods of history. This, however, is not to ignore that there have been others besides the Brahmavâdins in the historical period, who have spoken of the Thing in itself under such designations as 'The Absolute'. But, between them and the Brahmavâdin, there is a difference. While the conclusions of the former are professedly based on pure speculation, the latter stands alone as one who has spoken of the Thing in itself with that certainty which is born and bred of conviction produced by an immediate or intuitive cognition thereof. The whole literature of the Vedânta is devoted to an exposition of what Brahman, the Thing in itself, is, or rather what It is not. The truth of its teachings has been testified to by the personal experience of an unbroken line of teachers including S'rî-Gaudapâdâchârya and S'rí-S'ankarâchârya. Accordingly the Brahmavâdin concerns himself not only with the theory as to the nature of the Absolute, but also with the development of the faculty by which to come face to face with It. While logically establishing the nature of Brahman by an elaborate course of metaphysical argument, the Vedânta describes in some detail the process of purifying the mind or Manas as it is called. As Manas is purged of its dross, of its desires for and attachment to earthly and celestial pleasures, it loses its fickleness and tends to become steady. On attaining to a state of perfect steadiness, it ceases to be what it now appears to be and becomes one with Brahman; and this unity of Manas with Brahman is what is called *Brahma-Sâkshâtkâra*, an intuitive or immediate cognition of Brahman. Nothing short of the Sâkshâtkâra can produce an absolute conviction as to what the Thing in itself is.

With the Brahmavâdin, metaphysics is

nothing if it is not associated with religion; and in fact it forms the soul of his religion. His metaphysical conclusions form the groundwork of his religious devotion. The path of any particular religious devotee runs along the line of the conclusions his mind is capable of forming as to the nature of God, Soul and the Universe. No course of abstract contemplation of the Divine Being is recommended to one whose mind cannot rise to that level. Hence the multiform and apparently divergent paths of devotion recommended in the writings of the Aryan sages.

The Brahmavâdin's metaphysical philosophy derives its peculiarly religious significance from the fact of its being based on the direct experience of the enlightened sages who describe Brahman, the Absolute, as transcending in Its Bliss the highest reaches of human conception of happiness and pleasure. The Brahman of the Vedânta is at once the Absolute which the metaphysician strains his intellect to apprehend, the *summum bonum* which the moralist strives to attain by his acts, and the Divine Bliss which the ardent religious devotee aspires to realize in life by exclusive devotion to God with all his being. In fact, every orthodox Aryan system of science, art, and philosophy has its basis in religion and is calculated to subserve the interests of spiritual progress. Thus the Brahmavâdin affords a unique instance of a theologian, who has from the very dawn of his religion not learned to hate the light of truth thrown by the most astounding discoveries of science and the grandest conclusions of philosophy; who, on the other hand, has based the superstructure of his religion upon the deepest and the most far-reaching conclusions of all science and philosophy, nay upon nothing short of Divine Omniscient Wisdom.

The Brahmavâdin's theosophy is primarily founded on Revelation embodied in the scriptures known by the name of Upanishads and forming part of the Vedas. They are also known as the Vedânta, the last word of the Veda concerning what is called Vaidika-Dharma or Vedic Religion. It is not very easy to say exactly how many Upanishads there are. Tradition assigns one Upanishad to each Vedic school or S'âkhâ ; so that there being one-thousand-one-hundred-and-eighty Śâkhâs enumerated, there must be as many Upanishads in all. As most of the S'âkhâs are said to have become extinct, the Upanishads attached to them may have disappeared also.

Nevertheless, there are now found as many as one hundred and thirty or more Upanishads. Of these one hundred and odd Upanishads, only ten have been fully commented upon by S'rî-S'ankarâchârya, whose commentaries on Upanishads are the earliest extant. It is only these ten Upanishads and four others that have been cited as authorities by S'rî-S'ankarâchârya in his commentaries on Brahma-S'ûtras, and among them alone are those few that can be traced to the current Vedic schools. This fact as well as a striking difference in diction and subject-matter between these Upanishads and the rest has led some critics to regard the former alone as genuine Upanishads and the latter as mere imitations if not worse. Without, however, venturing the bold opinion that this view is altogether unfounded, one may still hold that even those Upanishads which Śrî-S'ankarâchârya has not commented upon or otherwise noticed may justly be allowed the title, as they conform to the accepted definition of the term. The great commentator derives the term from three words *upa* (near), *ni* (quite) and *sad* (to go, to perish, to waste away) and explains that the word means Brahma-vidyâ, the Spiritual Wisdom which, by leading its devotee very near to Brahman, brings about the final extinction of misery by eradicating it and burning up its very seed, *avidyâ*. And in this widest acceptation of the term, the title has been extended by later writers to such works as the Bhagavadgîtâ, which treat of Brahman and the means of attaining Divine Bliss. This elasticity in the application of the term does not altogether militate against the Brâhmanical doctrine of revelation; for, while holding that Vedas including Upanishads are eternal as embodying the eternal truths which, though not accessible to the mind of the ordinary man, are yet within the ken of the spiritual vision of the divine sages who can read them as it were recorded in the pages of superphysical nature, the orthodox Brâhmanism admits the possibility of sages and even the Divine Being revealing at different ages for the guidance of people so much of truth concerning transcendental matters as may be necessary for their spiritual progress, in the language of the people to whom the teaching is addressed. Unless, therefore, the application of the term is restricted to works of a particular age in the historical period, the title cannot be refused to the Upanishads in question. The settlement of the question as to how far they are genuine or authoritative must be made, in view of the foregoing considerations, to rest ultimately on the inherent truth of the teaching contained in each individual Upanishad, judged as all such cases are in the last resort by one's own intuition. But the fact that Śrî-Śankarânanda, who for many years occupied the apostolic seat of Śringeri Mutt (monastery) in the fourteenth century as the head of the most orthodox school of Aupanishadas (the followers of the Upanishads), has commented and otherwise discoursed upon many of those Upanishads which his great predecessor had left unnoticed, is enough to show that they form a valuable block of the sacred Scriptures, at least in so far as they have been made by religious teachers channels for conveying to their disciples spiritual instruction of no mean order. Śankarâchârya's omission to explain or otherwise notice them in his writings may be explained on the following ground. His main object was,—as may be seen from his attitude towards the various religious systems of his day which were too full of mischievous doctrines and corrupt practices under the cloak of devotion to a personal God or Goddess,—to purify them all by placing them on a rational basis. With this end in view, he concerned himself with the establishing of the essential principles of Universal Religion—of the Vaidika-Dharma or Wisdom-Religion—as treated of in the ten classical Upanishads and the Bhagavad-gîtâ. These writings supplemented by excerpts from four more Upanishads and from such other works as the Mahâbhârata, Vishnu-Purâna, Mânava-Dharmaśâstra which are least affected by predilections for any particular religion, afforded him ample materials for the laying of a common rational foundation of all religions. As to details in doctrine or practice connected with any particular religion, he was not opposed to anything which did not militate against the fundamental doctrines of the Vedic Religion.

The classical Upanishads have been translated into English by more than one scholar, and English translations of Śankarâchârya's commentaries on one or two of them have also been published. There is a near prospect of his commentaries on other Upanishads also being made available to the English-reading students. It is now proposed to publish with necessary comments English translations of the minor Upanishads,—in small volumes like the one now issued,—inasmuch as they throw much light upon the practical aspect of the Vedântic system of theosophy.

2

Among the many distinguishing features of the minor Upanishads two may be mentioned here: (1) a more detailed system of Yoga by which to realize the Unity established on the authority of the more classical Upanishads; (2) the sectarian character of most of them which treat of the Supreme Being in a particular aspect, as Śiva, Nârâyana, Ganapati, Krishna, Râma, Devî and so on, and which enjoin external practices and ceremonies which have become specially associated with particular sects. Both the Upanishads comprised in this volume are said to belong to the Atharva-veda and treat in some detail of the Yoga of meditation by which to realize the true nature of the Supreme Being. As regards the second characteristic mentioned above, the Amritabindu-upanishad may be said to be altogether free from any sectarian bias. The name 'Vâsudeva' occurring in the last verse of the Upanishad is not used in the same way that it is used in some of the sectarian Upanishads, Purânas, A'gamas and Tantras. But the Kaivalya-upanishad is held by the Śaivas as peculiarly favouring their doctrine of Śiva, the personal God, being identical with the Parabrahman and superior to other Gods such as Vishnu, Brahmâ, because of the occurrence of such terms as Śiva, Sadâśiva, Nîlakantha, Rudra, Umâ. These terms are, however, explained by some as applicable in their generic sense to the Supreme Being conceived in other forms. The followers of S'rî-Râmânujâchârya, for instance, who claim Supreme Divinity to the personal God Vishnu, explain these terms in their generic sense and apply them to Vishnu. To show that the Supreme Being is none of the personal Gods as such, others refer to the passage in which Śiva, Vishnu and all other personal Gods are mentioned as the manifestations of the One Existence which has no form. The peculiar merit, however, attached to the recitation of the S'atarudrîya text may be regarded as favouring to some extent the contention of the Śaivas. But even this argument loses much of its force if we take into consideration the difference of opinion among commentators as to what text is referred to in the Upanishad, as the S'atarudrîya (*vide* p. 71) ; the S'aivas holding that the section beginning with "*Namaste Rudra*" (Taittirîya-Samhitâ IV. v.) is particularly sacred as designating the Supreme Being in a special way. These considerations notwithstanding, the Kaivalya-Upanishad seems to contain within it the seed capable of developing into the S'aiva system of Religion as we now find it.

The notes accompanying the text of the Upanishads have been compiled from the well-known comments on Upanishads by S'ankarânanda and Nârâyanatîrtha. Sânkarânanda's comments on these and many other Upanishads, especially as found in his masterly expositions which go under the name of A'tmapurâna, are particularly valuable as embodying much information of a traditional character only vouchsafed by a well-informed teacher to the disciple. While discoursing on the teaching of the Amritabindu-Upanishad, he has made two extracts from Gaudapâda's Kârikâs on Mândûkyopanishad. To make clear the full meaning of these verses, it has been thought necessary to add to them S'ankarâchârya's commentaries thereon as expounded by A'nandagiri,—the bhâshya being too terse to be clearly understood without A'nandagiri's gloss. The real nature of Manas and the process of restraining it are so pointedly treated of by Gaudapâda in the verses quoted by S'ankarânanda that they have been accorded a place in the volume co-ordinate with that of the main Upanishad.

The two Upanishads under notice represent

the current orthodox Brâhmanism as founded on the teaching of the Upanishads. While maintaining that truth in the abstract and the ultimate aim of life is one and the same for all, Brâhmanism points out different paths to different classes of aspirants, each path being suited to the intellectual, moral and spiritual progress of those to whom it is recommended.

He whose mind is so well prepared by a long course of training in the previous incarnations as to realize at the first hearing the Vedântic teaching regarding the unity of the Self and Brahman and the evanescent nature of all else, —such a Mahâtman lives in the infinite Bliss of Brahman and has achieved the highest object of life.

It is others who are to walk in one or other of the various paths pointed out by the S'ruti. The one aim to be achieved in all these is the perfect purity and steadiness of Manas, which being attained, Brahman will shine forth in Its true nature in Manas The paths described in the following pages are these:

(1) *Contemplation of the Nirguna or Unconditioned Brahman*:—He alone is fit to enter on this path who is intellectually convinced of the reality of A'tman and the unreality of all else. In connection with this path a note of warning

is often sounded exhorting the aspirant of this class to contemplate Nirguna-Brahman, not as devoid of all characteristics, but as *Sat-Chit-A'nanda*, as Being, Consciousness and Bliss. To do this the aspirant has only to strip his own individual consciousness of all the limitations caused by the Upâdhis till it becomes one with the Universal Consciousness as he can conceive it. He has thus to transfer his own individuality to that of Brahman till all idea of separateness vanishes away, and to fix his consciousness there, never losing hold of it. In fullness of time this contemplation will lead to an intuitive realization of the True nature of the Absolute Brahman. Any attempt to contemplate Brahman at the initial stage as altogether unconditioned will be tantamount to the contemplation of the Chaotic Tamas—of Avyakta, of Prakriti—which, if pursued to the culminating point, would lead to Prakriti-laya or absorption in the universal nature, thus throwing back the soul's spiritual evolution almost to its starting point. It is from this point of view that Lord Śrî Krishna has recommended contemplation of Iśvara or Saguna-Brahman manifested in the Universe as the best for all aspirants excepting the perfected men called Sânkhyas who have had glimpses into the true nature of the Absolute Brahman as identical with their Highest Self and who are therefore never liable to confound the Nirguna-Brahman with the Avyakta or Prakriti.

(2) *Contemplation of Saguna* or *Conditioned Brahman* :—Brahman being viewed in relation to the Universe, as its Source and its Guide; as the all-pervading self-conscious Supreme Lord of the Universe, as immanent in every particle of the universe emanating from Him.

(3) *Contemplation of Saguna-Brahman as external to oneself* :—Brahman being conceived as distinct from the devotee and endued with the attributes of infinite knowledge, power, love, glory, &c., in their perfection. As the idea of perfection differs with individuals, no universality of conception can be expected among this class of aspirants. Though conceived and worshipped in ever so many ways, the Divine Being, who in Himself is one and the same, dispenses His Grace to all alike, just in the way they approach Him.

(4) *Symbolic contemplation* :—Those who cannot meditate upon Brahman in Himself, should have recourse to a symbol representing Him. The symbol may be a word such as Pranava; or it may be an image, mental or physical.

(5) *Performance of religious works without thoughts of reward*:—He who, owing to his attachment to things of the world, cannot fix his mind on one object should continue to perform unselfishly all the duties pertaining to his station in life, contemplating God at intervals of work and occupied in the recitation of sacred texts. In course of time, his mind will be prepared to enter on the path of meditation.

These are the different stages on the Nivritti-Mârga or the Path of Liberation. A pilgrim may commence his journey at any one of these stages. True unselfish single-hearted devotion to the Supreme Being will sooner or later lead him on through all the intermediate stages to the Ultimate Goal.

MYSORE,
27th August 1898. } A. M. S.

उपनिषत्.

विषयसूचिका.

आथर्वणोपनिषदां शान्तिपाठः.

॥ हरिः ओम् ॥

भद्रं कर्णेभिश्शृणुयाम देवाः ।
भद्रं पश्येमाक्षभिर्यजत्राः ।
स्थिरैरङ्गैस्तुष्टुवाꣳसस्तनूभिः ।
व्यशेम देवहितं यदायुः ॥

स्वस्ति न इन्द्रो वृद्धश्रवाः ।
स्वस्ति नः पूषा विश्ववेदाः ।
स्वस्ति नस्तार्क्ष्यो अरिष्टनेमिः ।
स्वस्ति नो बृहस्पतिर्दधातु ॥

ओं शान्तिः शान्तिः शान्तिः ॥

ॐ.

अमृतबिन्दूपनिषत्.

हरिः ओम्.

मनो हि द्विविधं प्रोक्तं शुद्धं चाशुद्धमेव च ।
अशुद्धं कामसङ्कल्पं शुद्धं कामविवर्जितम् ॥ १

मन एव मनुष्याणां कारणं बन्धमोक्षयोः ।
बन्धाय विषयासक्तं मुक्त्यै[1] निर्विषयं स्मृतम् ॥ २

यतो निर्विषयस्यास्य मनसो मुक्तिरिष्यते ।
अतो निर्विषयं नित्यं मनः कार्यं मुमुक्षुणा ॥ ३

निरस्तविषयासङ्गं संनिरुद्धं मनो हृदि ।
यदा यात्यात्मनो भावं तदा तत् परमं पदम् ॥*४

तावदेव निरोद्धव्यं यावद्धृदि गतं क्षयम् ।
एतद् ज्ञानं च ध्यानं च शेषो न्यायश्च[2] विस्तरः॥५

पाठान्तरं— [1]मुक्तं. [2]अतोऽन्यो ग्रन्थ.

*अत्रानुसन्धेयाः गौडपादभगवत्पादीयमाण्डूक्योपानिषत्कारिकाः ५मे पृष्ठे द्रष्टव्याः.

नैव चिन्त्यं न चाचिन्त्यं न चिन्त्यं चिन्त्यमेव तत् ।
पक्षपातविनिर्मुक्तं ब्रह्म सम्पद्यते तदा[1] ॥ ६

स्वरेण[2] सन्धयेद्योगमस्वरं भावयेत् परम् ।
अस्वरेणानु[3]भावेन भावो वाऽ[4]भाव इष्यते ॥ ७

तदेव निष्कलं ब्रह्म निर्विकल्पं निरञ्जनम् ।
तद्ब्रह्माहमिति ज्ञात्वा ब्रह्म सम्पद्यते ध्रुवम् ॥ ८
निर्विकल्पमनन्तं च हेतुदृष्टान्तवर्जितम् ।
अप्रमेयमनादिं च यद् ज्ञात्वा मुच्यते बुधः ॥ ९

न निरोधो न चोत्पत्तिर्न बद्धो न च साधकः ।
न मुमुक्षुर्न वै मुक्त इत्येषा परमार्थता ॥ १०
एक एवात्मा मन्तव्यो जाग्रत्स्वप्नसुषुप्तिषु ।
स्थानत्रयव्यतीतस्य पुनर्जन्म न विद्यते ॥ ११

एक एव हि भूतात्मा भूतेभूते व्यवस्थितः ।
एकधा बहुधा चैव दृश्यते जलचन्द्रवत् ॥ १२

घटसंवृतमाकाशं नीयमाने घटे यथा ।
घटो नीयेत नाकाशः तथा जी[5]वो नभोपमः ॥ १३

[1]ध्रुवं. [2]णा. [3]ण हि. [4]ना. [5]द्वज्जी.

घटवद्विविधाकारं भिद्यमानं पुनःपुनः ।
तद्भग्नं न च[1] जानाति स जानाति च नित्यशः* ॥

शब्दमायावृतो नैव तमसा[2] याति पुष्करे ।
भिन्ने तमसि चैकत्वमेक एवानुपश्यति ॥ १५

शब्दाक्षरं परं ब्रह्म तस्मिन् क्षीणे यदक्षरम् ।
तद्विद्वानक्षरं ध्यायेद्यदि[3] च्छेच्छान्तिमात्मनः ॥ १६

द्वे विद्ये वेदितव्ये तु शब्दब्रह्म परं च यत् ।
शब्दब्रह्मणि निष्णातः परं ब्रह्माधिगच्छति ॥ १७

ग्रन्थमभ्यस्य मेधावी ज्ञानविज्ञानतत्परः ।
पलालमिव धान्यार्थी त्यजेद्ग्रन्थमशेषतः ॥ १८

गवामनेकवर्णानां क्षीरस्याप्येकवर्णता ।
क्षीरवत् पश्यते ज्ञानं लिङ्गिनस्तु गवां यथा ॥ १९

घट[4]मिव पयासि निगूढं भूतेभूते वसति विज्ञानम् ।
सततं मन्थ भङ्ग मनसा[5] मन्थानभूतेन ॥ २०

---

[1] द्वेदे च न. [2] सो. [3] दी. [4] घृत.

[5] सततं मनासि मन्थयितव्यं मनो; सततं मनासि मन्थयितव्यं मनसा

*अत्रानुसन्धेया गौडपादकारिकाः ७मे पृष्ठे द्रष्टव्याः.

ज्ञाननेत्रं समादाय उ[1]द्धरेद् वह्निवत् परम्[2] ।
निष्कलं निश्चलं शान्तं तद् ब्रह्माहमिति स्मृतम् ॥ २१

सर्वभूताधिवासं यद् भूतेषु च वसत्यपि ।
सर्वानुग्राहकत्वेन तदस्म्यहं वासुदेवः ॥ २२

तदस्म्यहं वासुदेव इति ॥

इत्यथर्ववेदे अमृतबिन्दूपनिषत् समाप्ता ॥

——

गौडपादकारिकाः.

१. अद्वैतप्रकरणे—

* * *

यथा स्वप्ने द्वयाभासं स्पन्दते मायया मनः ।
तथा जाग्रद् द्वयाभासं स्पन्दते मायया मनः॥ २९

अद्वयं च द्वयाभासं मनः स्वप्ने न संशयः ।
अद्वयं च द्वयाभासं तथा जाग्रन्न संशयः ॥ ३०

मनोदृश्यमिदं द्वैतं यत्किञ्चित् सचराचरम् ।
मनसो ह्यमनीभावे द्वैतं नैवोपलभ्यते ॥ ३१

---

[1] चो.

[2] चेरद्वाह्निमतः परम्.

आत्मसत्यानुबोधेन न सङ्कल्पयते यदा ।
अमनस्तां तदा याति ग्राह्याभावे तदग्रहम् ॥ ३२

अकल्पकमजं ज्ञानं ज्ञेयाभिन्नं प्रचक्षते ।
ब्रह्म ज्ञेयमजं नित्यमजेनाजं विबुध्यते ॥ ३३

निगृहीतस्य मनसो निर्विकल्पस्य धीमतः ।
प्रचारः स तु विज्ञेयः सुषुप्तेऽन्यो न तत्समः ॥ ३४

लीयते हि सुषुप्ते तन्निगृहीतं न लीयते ।
तदेव निर्भयं ब्रह्म ज्ञानालोकं समन्ततः ॥ ३५

अजमनिद्रमस्वप्नमनामकमरूपकम् ।
सकृद्विभातं सर्वज्ञं नोपचारः कथंचन ॥ ३६

सर्वाभिलापविगतः सर्वचिन्तासमुत्थितः ।
सुप्रशान्तः सकृज्ज्योतिः समाधिरचलोऽभयः ॥ ३७

ग्रहो न तत्र नोत्सर्गश्चिन्ता यत्र न विद्यते ।
आत्मसंस्थं तदा ज्ञानमजाति समतां गतम् ॥ ३८

अस्पर्शयोगो वै नाम दुर्दर्शः सर्वयोगिभिः ।
योगिनो बिभ्यति ह्यस्मादभये भयदर्शिनः ॥ ३९

मनसो निग्रहायत्तमभयं सर्वयोगिनाम् ।
दुःखक्षयः प्रबोधश्चाप्यक्षया शान्तिरेव च ॥ ४०

उत्सेक उदधेर्यद्वत् कुशाग्रेणैकबिन्दुना ।
मनसो निग्रहस्तद्वद् भवेदपरिखेदतः ॥ ४१

उपायेन निगृह्णीयाद्विक्षिप्तं कामभोगयोः ।
सुप्रसन्नं लये चैव यथा कामो लयस्तथा ॥ ४२

दुःखं सर्वमनुस्मृत्य कामभोगान्निवर्तयेत् ।
अजं सर्वमनुस्मृत्य जातं नैव तु पश्यति ॥ ४३

लये सम्बोधयेच्चित्तं विक्षिप्तं शमयेत् पुनः ।
सकषायं विजानीयात् समप्राप्तं न चालयेत् ॥ ४४

नास्वादयेत् सुखं तत्र निस्सङ्गः प्रज्ञया भवेत् ।
निश्चलं निश्चरच्चित्तमेकीकुर्यात् प्रयत्नतः ॥ ४५

यदा न लीयते चित्तं न च विक्षिप्यते पुनः ।
अनिङ्गनमनाभासं निष्पन्नं ब्रह्म तत्तदा ॥ ४६

स्वस्थं शान्तं सनिर्वाणमकथ्यं सुखमुत्तमम् ।
अजमजेन ज्ञेयेन सर्वज्ञं परिचक्षते ॥ ४७

* * *

२. अलातशान्तिप्रकरणे—

* * *

ऋजुवक्रादिकाभासमलातस्पन्दितं यथा ।
ग्रहणग्राहकाभासं विज्ञानस्पन्दितं तथा ॥ ४७

अस्पन्दमानमलातमनाभासमजं यथा ।
अस्पन्दमानं विज्ञानमनाभासमजं तथा ॥ ४८

B

अलाते स्पन्दमाने वै नाभासा अन्यतोभुवः ।
न ततोऽन्यत्र निस्स्पन्दान्नालातं प्रविशन्ति ते ॥ ४९

न निर्गता अलातात्ते द्रव्यत्वाभावयोगतः ।
विज्ञानेऽपि तथैव स्युराभासस्याविशेषतः ॥ ५०

विज्ञाने स्पन्दमाने वै नाभासा अन्यतोभुवः ।
न ततोऽन्यत्र निस्स्पन्दान्न विज्ञानं विशन्ति ते ॥ ५१

न निर्गता विज्ञानात्ते द्रव्यत्वाभावयोगतः ।
कार्यकारणताभावाद्यतोऽचिन्त्याः सदैव ते ॥ ५२

* * *

कैवल्योपनिषत्.

हरिः ओम्.

अथाश्वलायनो भगवन्तं परमेष्ठिनमुप[1]समेत्यो-
वाच—

अधीहि भगवन् ब्रह्मविद्यां वरिष्ठां
सदा सद्भिः सेव्यमानां निगूढाम् ।
ययाऽचिरात् सर्वपापं व्यपोह्य
परात् परं पुरुषं या[2]ति विद्वान् ॥ १

तस्मै स होवाच पितामहश्च
श्रद्धाभक्तिध्यानयोगादवेहि ।
न कर्मणा न प्रजया धनेन
त्यागेनैके अमृतत्वमानशुः ॥ २

परेण नाकं निहितं गुहायां
वि[3]भ्राजते यद्यतयो विशन्ति ।

---

[1] नं परि, [2] रुषमुपै. [3] बि.

वेदान्तविज्ञानसुनिश्चितार्थाः
संन्यासयोगाद्यतयः शुद्धसत्त्वाः ॥ ३

ते ब्रह्मलोकेषु परान्तकाले
परामृतात् परिमुच्यन्ति सर्वे ।
विविक्तदेशे च सुखासनस्थः
शुचिः समग्रीवशिरश्शरीरः ॥ ४

अत्याश्रमस्थः सकलेन्द्रियाणि
निरुध्य भक्त्या स्वगुरुं प्रणम्य ।
हृत्पुण्डरीकं विरजं विशुद्धं
विचिन्त्य मध्ये विशदं विशोकम् ॥ ५

अचिन्त्यमव्यक्तमनन्तरूपं
शिवं प्रशान्तममृतं ब्रह्मयोनिम् ।
तथाऽऽ[1]दिमध्यान्तविहीनमेकं
विभुं चिदानन्दमरूपमद्भुतम् ॥ ६

उमासहायं परमेश्वरं प्रभुं
त्रिलोचनं नीलकण्ठं प्रशान्तम् ।

---

[1]दा.

ध्यात्वा मुनिर्गच्छति भूतयोनिं
समस्तसाक्षिं तमसः परस्तात् ॥ ७

स ब्रह्मा स शिवः सेन्द्रः सोऽक्षरः परमः स्वराट् ।
स एव विष्णुः स प्राणः स कालोऽ[1]ग्निः स चन्द्रमाः ॥

स एव सर्वं यद्भूतं यच्च भव्यं[2] सनातनम् ।
ज्ञात्वा तं मृत्युमत्येति नान्यः पन्था विमुक्तये ॥ ९

सर्वभूतस्थमात्मानं सर्वभूतानि चात्मनि ।
सम्पश्यन् ब्रह्म परमं याति नान्येन हेतुना ॥ १०

आत्मानमरणिं कृत्वा प्रणवं चोत्तरारणिम् ।
ज्ञा[3]ननिर्मथनाभ्यासात् पाशं दहति पण्डितः ॥ ११

स एव मायापरिमोहितात्मा
शरीरमास्थाय करोति सर्वम् ।
स्त्रय[4]न्नपानादिविचित्रभोगैः
स एव जाग्रत् परितृप्तिमेति ॥ १२

---

[1]ला. [2]सर्वं. [3]ध्या. [4]स्त्रिय.

स्वप्ने स[1] जीवः सुखदुःखभोक्ता
स्वमायया कल्पितविश्वलोके ।
सुषुप्तिकाले सकले विलीने
तमोऽभिभूतः सुखरूपमेति ॥
पुनश्च जन्मान्तरकर्मयोगात्
स एव जीवः स्वपिति प्रबुद्धः ॥ १३

पुरत्रये क्रीडति यश्च[2] जीवः
ततस्तु जातं सकलं विचित्रम् ।
आधारमानन्दमखण्डबोधं
यस्मिन् लयं याति पुरत्रयं च ॥ १४

एतस्माज्जायते प्राणो मनः सर्वेन्द्रियाणि च ।
खं वायुर्ज्योतिरापः पृथिवी विश्वस्य धारिणी ॥ १५

यत् परं ब्रह्म सर्वात्मा विश्वस्यायतनं महत् ।
सूक्ष्मात् सूक्ष्मतरं नित्यं तत्त्वमेव त्वमेव तत् ॥ १६

जाग्रत्स्वप्नसुषुप्त्यादि प्रपञ्चं यत् प्रकाशते ।
तद् ब्रह्माहमिति ज्ञात्वा सर्वबन्धैः प्रमुच्यते ॥ १७

---

[1]तु; ऽपि [2]स्तु.

त्रिषु धामसु यद् भोग्यं भोक्ता भोगश्च यद् भवेत् ।
तेभ्यो विलक्षणः साक्षी चिन्मात्रोऽहं सदाशिवः ॥ १८

मय्येव सकलं जातं मयि सर्वं प्रतिष्ठितम् ।
मयि सर्वं लयं याति तद् ब्रह्माद्वयमस्म्यहम् ॥ १९

अणोरणीयानहमेव तद्वत्
महानहं विश्वमिदं विचित्रम् ।
पुरातनोऽहं पुरुषोऽहमीशो
हिरण्मयोऽहं शिवरूपमस्मि ॥ २०

अपाणिपादोऽहमचिन्त्यशक्तिः
पश्याम्यचक्षुः स[1]शृणोम्यकर्णः ।
अहं विजानामि विविक्तरूपो
न चास्ति वेत्ता मम चित् सदाऽहम् ।
वेदैरनेकैरहमेव वेद्यो
वेदान्तकृद्वेदविदेव चाहम् ॥ २१

न पुण्यपापे मम नास्ति नाशो
न जन्म देहेन्द्रियबुद्धिरस्ति ।

---

[1]सु.

न भूमिरापो न च[1] वह्निरस्ति
न चानिलो मेऽस्ति न चाम्बरं च ॥ २२

एवं विदित्वा परमात्मरूपं
गुहाशयं निष्कलमद्वितीयम् ।
समस्तसाक्षिं सदसद्विहीनं
प्रयाति शुद्धं परमात्मरूपम् ॥ २३

इति प्रथमः खण्डः.

यः शतरुद्रीयमधीते सोऽग्निपूतो भवति[2] सुरा-
पानात् पूतो भवति ब्रह्महत्यात् पूतो भवति कृत्याकृ-
त्यात् पूतो भवति तस्मादविमुक्तमाश्रितो भवति ।
अत्याश्रमी सर्वदा सकृद्वा जपेत् ॥ १

अनेन ज्ञानमाप्नोति संसारार्णवनाशनम् ।
तस्मादेवं विदित्वैनं कैवल्यं फलमश्नुते ॥ २

कैवल्यं फलमश्नुत इति ॥

इति द्वितीयः खण्डः.

इत्यथर्ववेदे कैवल्योपनिषत् समाप्ता.

---

[1] मम. [2] "स्वर्णस्तेयात्पूतो भवति" इत्याधिकः पाठः.

THE

A'THARVANA-UPANISHADS.

S'A'NTI-PA'ṬHA

OR

THE PEACE-CHANT.

Om.

What is auspicious with our ears may we hear, O Gods. With our eyes may we see what is auspicious, always engaged in worship. Adoring with organs and bodies perfect, may we enjoy the length of life granted us by the Gods.

May the wise-taught Indra grant us welfare. May the all-knowing Pûshan grant us welfare. May Târkshya of unfailing wheel grant us welfare. May Brihaspati grant us welfare.

Om! Peace! Peace!! Peace!!!

The two mantras here cited are chanted when beginning the study of an upanishad belonging to the Atharvaveda.

Wise-taught: taught by the Divine Sage Bṛihaspati. *Pûshan*: literally *nourisher*; generally applied to the sun. *Târkshya*: "the name of a mythical being described either as a horse or as a bird, and originally one of the personifications of the sun, which was represented under these forms." Târkshya is explained by Bhattabhâskara to mean a vehicle (ratha) made of metres (chhandases). The word is sometimes treated as synonymous with *Garuda*, the Divine Bird whereon God Vishnu rides. Garuda is very probably a symbolic representation of Time, either directly, or indirectly through the sun. *Bṛihaspati*: the name of a deity who may be regarded as Piety and Religion personified...He is the type of the priestly order and is represented as the chief priest of the Gods.

I.

AMṚITABINDU-UPANISHAD

WITH

COMMENTS.

AMRITABINDU-UPANISHAD.

Introduction.

This upanishad is said to belong to the Atharvaveda and is known by two names, *Amṛita-bindu* and *Brahma-bindu*, meaning "a small work treating of the immortal Brahman;" or, "a treatise of which every syllable is like a drop of nectar." It is chiefly intended to reveal how best to attain to Brahma-sâkshâtkâra, to an intuitive recognition of Brahman as identical with one's own Self. The best process, the one which lies at the root of all others, the type of which those others are more or less imperfect specimens, is said to consist in *mano-nirodha*, the restraint of all the internal and external—subjective and objective—wanderings of the manas till it ceases to be what it appears to be and attains to its true being, which is nothing but Brahman, the Bliss. This state is called samâdhi.

The conclusion of all upanishads may be summed up thus: by a knowledge of the identity of Jîva or the individual Self with Brahman, cessation of all evil may be brought about and Spiritual Bliss attained. And this Brahma-jñâna can be acquired by an enquiry into the teaching of the upanishads, followed by reflection and contemplation thereof, which require again the aid of manas. Manas is, like a wild elephant, very hard for men to control, and it is therefore first taken up for treatment in this upanishad.

Pure and impure manas.

1. Manas, verily, is said to be twofold, pure and impure; the impure one is that which has thoughts of objects of desire (Kâma), and the pure one that which is free from desire (Kâma).

Manas is the antaḥ-karana, the inner sense, which undergoes various modifications called vṛittis. The wise say that it is twofold, pure and impure. Impure as it generally is, it is rendered pure by the innumerable acts of righteousness (punya) done in the past, by Brahmacharya (physical and mental chastity), by upâsana or meditation and other such observances in the present birth. Manas is said to be impure when it is full of desire, when it thinks of objects of desire. When it is altogether free from desire, manas is said to be pure. Sometimes it is neither quite pure nor quite impure; and sometimes it is quite dull and inactive.

Manas the cause of bondage and liberation.

Now the question arises : what is the evil of the manas being impure, or what is the good of its being pure ? The answer follows :

2. Manas, verily, is the cause of bondage and liberation of men : engrossed in objects (it leads) to bondage ; free from objects (it leads) to liberation : so they say.

The antaḥ-karana is the cause of bondage (bandha) and liberation (mukti) in the case of all of us, the children of Manu. Bondage consists in the egoistic thought of 'I' and 'mine' and their cause; and liberation consists in the manifestation in ourselves of the self-luminous Bliss or Átman, in the Átman manifesting Himself in His true nature. When manas is engrossed in the objects of sense—in food and drink and other carnal pleasures, in sound, touch, colour, taste, smell—with a longing desire, it causes bondage. When manas is free from a longing for the sense-objects mentioned above, it leads to liberation. Thus by *anvaya* and *vyatireka*, by what is called the method of agreement and difference, we find that pure manas conduces to moksha. So, too, do the wise people think.

Manas should be completely restrained from objects.

Every one should strive to render manas *nirvishaya*, to set it free from sense-objects :

3. Since liberation is ensured to this manas (when) free from objects, therefore by the seekers of liberation should the manas be ever made free from objects.

This: Manas is *Sâkshi-pratyaksha*, ever directly present before Átman, the Witness. We are ever conscious of the existence of manas. Mukti consists in liberation from such bonds as avidyâ; *i.e.*, mukti is attained when manas is dissolved or merged in the heart-lotus, when it attains to what is called *unmanî-bhâva* or *nis-sankalpatâ* state, the state in which there is no thought whatever in the manas. It is the condition known also as *manonmanî*, that state in which there reigns a perfect steadiness of manas.

Nirodha leads to liberation.

The result of such a nirodha or restraint of manas is stated as follows:

4. When manas, free from engrossment of objects, well restrained in the heart, attains to the A'tman's being, then it is the supreme abode.

Manas, when completely restrained in the heart-lotus, attains to the Átman's being, *i.e.*, it attains to a consciousness of the identity of Jîva and Brahman, to the consciousness that "I am Brahman". This attaining to the Átman's state is the result of the restraint of manas. Than this there is, indeed, nothing higher to be attained.

Sri Gaudapadacharya's exposition of mano-nirodha.

In this connection, a study of S'rî-Gaudapâdâchârya's exposition, in the *Advaitaprakarana* (a section of his commentary on the Mândûkya-upanishad), of the process of *mano-nirodha* which leads to the attainment of A'tman's real being may be found very instructive. Before describing the actual process he proves, by reasoning from experience, the declaration of the S'ruti that A'tman is all and that therefore manas has no real existence except as A'tman.

Emanation of Duality from the One Sat.

With this end in view the A'chârya proceeds to establish the emanation of the dual universe from the one *Sat* or Absolute Existence. In the section above referred to, he says :

"As in svapna manas acts by mâyâ, as though it were dual, so in the jâgrat, manas acts by mâyâ as though it were dual." (verse 29).

It is, indeed, held by philosophers that it is the manas regarded as an independent entity that transforms itself into the whole world of duality as experienced in the jâgrat and svapna states, in our waking and dream consciousness. The fact, however, is somewhat different. It is the Sat, Brahman, Átman Himself that, by mâyâ, emanates into various forms of being including manas. And manas itself is nothing but the Sat, as it is but a mere appearance of Brahman. Where a rope, for example, is mistaken for a serpent, the serpent has a real existence only when seen as identical with the rope. So also manas exists only in the sense in which it is identical with Átman, with the Absolute Consciousness which alone is the Supreme Reality, and on which the whole superstructure of manas with all its modifications is based.

Manifestation of the One as many.

It may be here asked, how can manas, identical with the one Sat or Átman, transform itself into the whole Universe ? This question can be answered by an appeal to the svapna state, in which the one manas is found to transform itself into various forms of being, into the percipient and the various objects of perception. It is admitted by all philosophers that the dual world which presents itself to consciousness in dream is a mere illusory creation of mâyâ, just as the serpent is an illusory appearance of the rope. In the jâgrat state as much as in the svapna state, it is by mâyâ that manas transforms itself into various forms of being.

Manas identical with Atman.

It should not be supposed that we have thus admitted two causes of the universe, *manas* and *Brahman*. For, as we have already pointed out, manas is but an illusory manifestation of A'tman, just as the serpent is an illusory manifestation of the rope, and as such it is really identical with A'tman and is therefore one and secondless. The A'châryа says :—

"And the non-dual manas appears, no doubt, as dual in svapna; so, too, the non-dual appears, no doubt, as dual in jâgrat." (verse 30).

It is manas indeed which manifests itself as the whole seeming duality of svapna. In the svapna state, as everybody is aware, there really exists nothing but vijñâna or consciousness; there neither exist the objects perceived such as elephants, nor are the eye and other organs of perception awake by which to perceive them. So, too, in the jâgrat or waking state, manas which is one and identical with A'tman, the only absolutely Real Being, manifests itself as senses and sense-objects. Thus, manas is only an illusory manifestation resting upon vijñâna or consciousness, inasmuch as consciousness alone is absolutely real, being present alike in the jâgrat and svapna states without any change whatever. And it is the manas of this sort,—that is, the manas which is really identical with Átman,—that presents itself in the form of all this dual world. Hence no plurality of causes.

Evidence that duality is nothing but manas.

It may be asked, what evidence is there to show that manas alone differentiates itself into the world of duality and is rooted in mere avidyâ or ignorance of the reality, like a rope manifesting itself by illusion as a serpent? The question is thus answered:

"Seen by manas is this duality, whatever is moving or unmoving; in non-mânasic state of manas, duality is not at all perceived." (verse 31).

The proposition is proved by resorting to anumâna or inference in its two aspects, *anvaya* and *vyatireka*, positive and negative. When manas undergoes differentiation, this world of duality is perceived. This constitutes the anvaya or positive proof, as in the following case of inferential evidence: only when clay is present do we perceive the jar, which, therefore, in its essence is no more than mere clay. The proposition to be proved here is that the whole duality is manas and manas only ; and the proof adduced is that the world exists only when manas exists.

The negative proof is of the following form: when there is no manas, there is no world of duality. This negative aspect of inferential evidence is indicated by a reference to the following facts of experience. In samâdhi manas becomes no-manas; it attains to the state called *amanîbhâva*. It is then completely restrained from its subjective and objective oscillations and thus reduced to no-manas by *vairâgya* or indifference to worldly objects, by constant meditation, and by the discriminative knowledge as to what is real and what is unreal. Where, for instance, a rope is mistaken for a serpent, the serpent is reduced to no-serpent by the knowledge of what it really is. In sushupti or dreamless sleep manas attains to *laya* or dissolution. In samâdhi and sushupti alike the world of duality is not perceived. And whatever is not perceived cannot be said to exist. *Meya* or an object of perception can be said to exist only when we perceive it: *mânâdhînâ meyasiddhiḥ*. Thus in samâdhi and sushupti in which no manas exists, the world of duality is not perceived and does not therefore exist.

What is meant by "manas becomes no-manas."

The foregoing statement may be objected to on the ground that, though not experienced in samâdhi and sushupti, manas does exist even in those states, inasmuch as manas is real in itself and always exists. This objection is answered as follows:

"When by the conviction of Átman's reality, manas imagines no more, then it becomes no-manas, unperceiving for want of objects of perception." (verse 32).

A'tman alone is real, as shewn by the S'ruti referring to clay as an example:

"All changing forms are mere names, a mere word of mouth; what we call clay is alone real." * Just as clay is alone admitted to be real, being constant in jars and all other earthen vessels which are unreal, so it should be admitted that A'tman alone is real, existing as he does in all objects that are looked upon as non-A'tman. When this truth is brought home to the mind by the teachings of the S'âstras and the A'chârya, manas, owing to the non-existence or unreality of the objects of thought, no longer thinks of them. In the absence, for instance, of fuel, fire can no longer burst into flame. Then, in the absence of objects of perception, manas no longer undergoes differentiation in the form of perceiver, perception and objects of perception, and thus comes to be no-manas.

To our ordinary thinking, in vyavahâra, manas is

* Chhândogya-Upanishad 6-1-4.

manas only as made of *sankalpas*, of thoughts and imaginings. These thoughts depend for their existence upon objects of thought, and the former cannot therefore exist in the absence of the latter. When the conviction arises that all is Átman and Átman only, then, owing to non-existence of objects of thought, manas no longer continues to be manas. That which then shines forth as consciousness is nothing but Átman. Thus, in the eye of one who is endued with discrimination, what we call manas does not exist.

Brahman is the Absolute self-luminous Consciousness.

When manas, whereof the existence is due to illusion (bhrama), thus becomes no-manas, *i.e.*, when it ceases to exist, *i.e.*, again, when it is known to be unreal, then there remains Átman alone freed from manas. This state is described by sages as follows :

> "Without any more imaginings, unborn, is knowledge inseparate from the Knowable, they declare. Brahman the knowable (it is), unborn and eternal. By the unborn the Unborn knows." (verse 33).

Then there remains knowledge which is not given to any imagining, and which is therefore unborn, *i.e.*, not subject to birth or other changes to which all phenomenal beings are subject. This knowledge which is mere consciousness is, as the Brahmavâdins declare, none other than Brahman, the Absolute Reality. Indeed, the knowledge of the Knower never fails, like the heat of fire never fails. Accordingly, the S'rutis declare: "Brahman is Knowledge and Bliss,"* "Reality, knowledge and infinite is Brahman."† In that knowledge itself is Brahman the knowable: it is inseparable from Brahman as heat is inseparable from fire. Since it is unborn, it is eternal (nitya) ever-existent.

One may object to this as follows: If all duality including manas be unreal or non-existent, then there remains nothing by which A'tman can be known, and therefore no knowledge of A'tman is possible. The S'ruti, however, says that "It can be seen by manas only."‡ And manas has been said to be unreal or non-existent.

This objection is anticipated by the sage who says that "by the unborn the Unborn knows." The residual knowledge has been shewn to be unborn, and this unborn knowledge is the essence of A'tman. By that knowledge, the Unborn—the A'tman that has to be known—knows Himself. A'tman is one mass, as it were, made up solely of vijñâna or consciousness in essence, just as the sun is essentially a mass of unfailing light. A'tman is consciousness itself. A'tman does not stand in need of external

---

* Brihadâranyaka-upanishad, 3-9-28. † Taittirîya-upanishad, 2-1. ‡ Brihadâranyaka-upanishad, 4-4-19.

knowledge to shine forth. That is to say, by that consciousness alone which is inherent in His essence, a knowledge of A'tman is possible; no such thing as manas external to Him is required for the purpose.

Amanibhava not identcial with Sushupti.

It should not be supposed that, owing to the absence in it of all acts of thought, samâdhi is the same as sushupti. For,

"The behaviour of manas thus restrained,—freed from imagining and endued with wisdom,—is clearly perceived (by yogins); in sushupti it is different; it is not the same as that." (verse 34).

We have said above:—When convinced of the grand truth that A'tman alone is real, as has been shown above, there remains no external object which manas may think of. Having nothing to think of in the absence of external objects, manas ceases to think altogether. Like fire having no fuel to feed upon, manas grows tranquil. Then it is said to become *niruddha*, completely restrained and neutralized; it is said to have attained to samâdhi. And it has been further said that when manas becomes no-manas, the Dvaita or Duality which is but manas in motion, is absent.

Thus, when manas is possessed of *viveka,* of the conviction that A'tman alone is real and the rest unreal, it becomes thoroughly restrained, and freed from all imaginings owing to the absence of all objects of thought. Manas then gets resolved into Pratyagâtman, the Innermost Self. This peculiar behaviour of manas is familiar only to the yogins; it is *vidvatpratyaksha*, it is intuitively known only to the wise sages, only to the Illuminate.

(*Objection*:)—Since all cognition is absent alike in sushupti and nirodha states, the behaviour of manas in the nirodha state is the same as in sushupti state, *i.e.*, the behaviour of manas in *nirodha* is quite as far beyond consciousness as that in *sushupti*, and therefore in the nirodha state there remains nothing of which the yogin may become conscious.

(*Answer*:)—The behaviour of manas in the nirodha state is quite distinct from its behaviour in the sushupti state.

Wherein lies the difference between the two.

In the sushupti state, manas is embraced by *avidyâ*, by *delusion*, by the *Tamas*,* and is pregnant

* These three terms, *Avidyâ*, *Moha*, and *Tamas* are descriptive designations of one and the same thing, showing that what is called Avidyâ is not a mere negative of Vidyâ, *i.e.*, the mere absence of Vidyâ, nor is it a mere hallucination of the mind (*chitta-bhrama*). It is, on the other hand, a distinct principle called Tamas or Darkness, far subtler than *chitta* or the thinking principle; and it is that extremely thin veil which envelops the Absolute Reality.

with vâsanâs or tendencies which, concealed within manas, are the source of all the activities that lead to many an evil result; whereas, in the nirodha state, avidyâ and all other seeds of activity leading to many an evil result are burnt up by the fire of the conviction that A'tman alone is real, and all Rajas giving rise to all sorts of pain is perfectly neutral. Manas, is then in its own state, quite independent, having attained to Brahman's own state of being. Thus, the behaviour of manas in the nirodha state is quite distiuct from that in the sushupti state. And though very hard to know, it is a thing which one may realise in consciousness.

Thus liberation, the result of jñâna, is not a remote (paroksha) result like svarga resulting from karma performed here. It is as immediately experienced as the sense of satisfaction immediately following the act of eating. The result of jñâna consists, as here described, in *mano-nirodha* which, as has been shewn above, follows closely upon jñâna and becomes a fact of experience.

Gaudapâda describes the difference between sushupti and samâdhi as follows:

"In sushupti, manas attains laya; when restrained it does not attain laya. That alone is the fearless Brahman, luminous with knowledge all around. It is unborn, sleepless, dreamless, nameless, formless, ever-luminous, omniscient. No ceremony whatever." (verses 35-36.)

In sushupti manas attains laya, *i. e.*, is resolved into its seed, its primal cause, the chaotic unconscious principle of Tamas,—along with all the vâsanâs, the tendencies or latent impressions of avidyâ * and other seeds of affliction. In the nirodha state, on the other hand, manas is restrained in virtue of its discriminative knowledge, in virtue of the conviction that Átman alone is real. It does not attain laya ; it is not resolved into its seed, the chaotic Tamas ; it does not exist even in the subtlest form, in the form of its cause. Wherefore it is but right to say that the behaviour of manas is different in the nirodha and sushupti states.

---

* The five afflictions are thus enumerated and defined by Patanjali in his Yoga-Sutras ii. 3—9 :

(1) *Avidyâ* or *Ignorance :* The mistaking of what is non-eternal, impure, painful, and non-self to be eternal, pure, joyous and self.

(2) *Asmitâ* or *Egoism* : the identifying of the seer with the act of seeing.

(3) *Râga* or *Desire* : a longing for pleasure or for the cause of pleasure.

(4) *Dvesha* or *Aversion* : a dislike for pain or for the cause of pain.

(5) *Abhiniveśa* or *Tenacity of life* : a strong natural desire to live, cherished even by the wise.

Nirodha state described.

When manas, brought into samâdhi state, is rid of the twofold dirt caused by avidyâ,—the dirt of perception and the dirt of organs of perception,—manas becomes the very Brahman, supreme, secondless. That, therefore, is verily the fearless—since there exists no perception of duality which is the cause of fear—tranquil Brahman, which being known man has none to fear. It shines forth as jñâna (consciousness) which is the essential nature of A'tman; that is to say, A'tman is one solid mass, as it were, made up solely of consciousness, pervading all around, like the âkâśa or ether. It is the very Brahman. It is the unborn: it has, indeed, been said that avidyâ is the cause of all birth. When a rope, for example, is mistaken for a serpent, it is certainly avidyâ that has given rise to the birth of the serpent in the rope. And this avidyâ has been removed by the conviction that A'tman alone is real. Avidyâ, which is the cause of all brith, being thus absent in the nirodha state, that which then persists and shines forth is not subject to birth, either within or without. For the same reason that it is unborn—*i. e.*, because there is no avidyâ—It is *anidra*, without *nidrâ*; for, nidrâ here denotes avidyâ itself, the beginningless mâyâ. It is *asvapna*, sleepless, as having completely awakened from the sleep of mâyâ and become the non-dual Átman. It is *nameless* and *formless*: Brahman is not designated by name nor represented to be of this or that form. The S'ruti says :— "From whom all words as well as manas return, having failed to reach Him."* Name and form applied to us are products of mere ignorance. By knowledge they have been extinguished; just as, where a rope has been mistaken for a serpent, the serpent has been extinguished by knowledge. It is, moreover, *ever-luminous*. It is light ever shining; for, It is never unperceived nor misperceived; It neither comes into manifestation nor goes out of sight. It is said to be unperceived when no consciousness that 'I am' arises in Jîva or the individual Self associated with upâdhi (avidyâ); then A'tman goes out of sight. When there arises in the same Jîva the consciousness that 'I am the agent,'—when the Átman is wrongly perceived,—then Átman is said to come into manifestation. As manifestation and disappearance of this kind are alike absent in Brahman, It is ever-effulgent.

Now an objector may say :—Before Brahman is taught by S'ruti or Áchârya, It is said to be unperceived, and after It has been taught, It is said to be perceived. Thus Brahman is subject to perception and non-perception.

We answer :—Not so; for, perception and non-perception are like day and night. As to the sun

* Taittirîya-upanishad, 2-4.

considered in himself, there can be neither day nor night; they are pure imaginations, born of another illusory notion that the sun rises and sets. So also, in Brahman considered in Itself there can be no perception or non-perception; they are mere imaginations due to upâdhi: Brahman without upâdhi is ever-effulgent.

Moreover, Tamas which is of the nature of avidyâ or ignorance is the cause of Brahman's not being ever-effulgent to us. From the standpoint of Brahman there can be no connection whatever with Tamas; and in itself Brahman is the eternal, ever-effulgent consciousness. For the same reason, Brahman is All and is Himself the Knower

The wise man whose manas has attained to nirodha, and who therefore has attained to the state of Brahman, has nothing more to do. With regard to the nirupâdhika or unconditioned Brahman, no formal worship is necessary. He alone who has not realised A'tman has to resort to samâdhi and other forms of worship, by which to approach the Divine Being regarded as external to himself. Brahman being ever-Existent, Pure, Conscious, and Free, for the wise man whose avidyâ has been extinguished and who has himself become Brahman, there can be nothing whatever to do.

All vyavahâra or action in general exists only in the state of avidyâ; in the state of vidyâ or enlightenment, avidyâ is entirely absent, and therefore no vyavahâra can exist. A mere semblance, however, of vyavahâra is possible, owing to a temporary continuance of what has been found to be unreal.

Brahman is none other than the wise man in the nirodha state.

The A'chârya describes the wise man who has attained samâdhi in the following words:

"Free from all speech, having risen above all thought, perfectly serene, ever-effulgent, the samâdhi, immutable, fearless." (Verse 37.)

It has been said that what shines forth in the nirodha state has no name and form, and so on. It has then no organ of speech—the source of names of all kinds—or any other external organ of sensation. It has risen above all thought: It has then no buddhi, no antaḥ-karana by which to think. It is thus quite pure. There exists not in It even a trace of these, not even their cause, avidyâ, in its subtlest form. As devoid of all objects of perception, It is perfectly serene. It is ever-effulgent as the self-conscious A'tman. It is spoken of as samâdhi because It is attainable by the prajñâ or consciousness which results from samâdhi, or because It is the Supreme A'tman in whom Jîva (the individual) and his upâdhi find their resting place. It is immutable and therefore fearless. This state of nirodha-samâdhi is attainable only as the result of a vast amount of good karma.

Nirodha marks the end of the Path.

On attaining to *nirodha-samâdhi*, nothing more remains to be done, as the Áchârya says :

"No taking or giving up is there where no thought exists. Centred in Átman then is knowledge, without birth, having attained equality." (Verse. 38).

Because Brahman alone shines forth in the nirodha state and is spoken of as immutable and fearless, therefore in that state, *i.e.*, in Brahman, there can be neither taking nor giving up. Where there is change or liability to change, there alone taking and giving up are possible ; but neither of the two can exist in Brahman. There can be no change in Brahman because there is no second thing which can cause change ; and there can be no liability to change, because Brahman has no parts. In Brahman there can be no thought of any. kind. When manas has thus ceased to be manas, how can there be taking or giving up ? On the rise of the conviction that A'tman alone is real, then, in the absence of all objects of perception, consciousness (jnâna) becomes centered in Átman alone, just as heat becomes centred in fire itself when there is no fuel to burn. Such a consciousness is birthless and has attained to absolute identity.

Thus it has been shewn how Brahman which is immutable and present ever and everywhere is really unborn, though by illusion It appears to be this thing now and that thing at another time. Compared with the conviction that Átman alone is real, all else is low and mean. On attaining to this knowledge, a brâhman has achieved all and has nothing more to do.

Few can reach Nirodha.

Thus, Brahman, the Supreme Reality, the Inner Self, the Immutable (kûtastha), Existence (sat), Intelligence (chit) and Bliss (ânanda) is attainable by a knowledge of the Reality, by a firm conviction of Its non-duality. Still the self-complacent unenlightened men do not apply themselves to it. Of this class of people the A'châry̦a says :

"Unstained Yoga, verily, is this called, hard to see for all yogins. Yogins, indeed, are afraid of this, seeing fear in the Fearless." (Verse 39.)

Nirodha is well known in the upanishads by the name of *untainted* (asparśa) *yoga*, as untouched by, or unrelated to, anything whatever : it is *asparśa* or *untainted* because of the very intuitive experience of non-dual A'tman in virtue of which neither the merit (dharma) of caste and religious order nor the dirt of sin can affect the soul ; and it is *yoga* because Jîva is thereby united to Brahman. It is very hard for a yogin to attain,—for him who does not possess vedântic wisdom. A yogin attains it only after undergoing a good deal of trouble involved in the processes of *śravana*, *manana* and *nididhyâsana*, *i.e.*, of learning the ancient wisdom from the Teacher, and of reflecting and contemplating thereon, and so on,—the processes by which alone one can attain to the conviction that A'tman alone is real.

Self-deluded Karma-Yogins.

The real nature of the Supreme Brahman is very hard for yogins to realize,—for those devotees who work in the path of Karma with their vision always directed to the external world. They are afraid of the nirodha-yoga, though it is free from all taint of evil.

These followers of vedic ritual look upon this samâdhi—this knowledge of the Reality—with great fear as leading to mere self-extinction, thinking that thereby they would lose their brâhman caste and all. They are unwise, being given to imagining fear of self-extinction where there is really no fear at all: knowledge of Reality is indeed the very means of attaining to fearless state.

Like men born blind, these yogins always engrossed as they are in matters external, do not see and realize their own real Self; they declare that amanîbhâva or samâdhi is allied to sushupti. The first cause of their fear is ajñâna which gives rise to many an illusory phenomenon. Next, born of this illusion come the manifold groundless hypotheses.

Self-deluded Sa'nkhyas.

Those yogins, for instance, who follow the Sânkhya system of philosophy hold as follows: It cannot be that one A'tman alone exists in all beings without any distinction, nor that He is essentially composed of mere Intelligence and Bliss. Since in our experience we find happiness and misery differently allotted to different beings, the Átmans (Purushas) must be different in different bodies. The Prakṛiti which is the cause of the Purushas' enjoyment and suffering is one only. They explain the behaviour of Prakṛiti in moksha in various alternative ways:

(1). Though one and common to all Purushas, Prakṛiti manifests Itself in many a form and vanishes altogether in mukti.

(2). Though in bondage Prakṛiti is what we find It to be, evolving into many a form, from the subtlest to the grossest ones, yet in mukti It retraces back Its steps and withdraws—or becomes resolved—into Its own primeval form.

(3). The cause of bondage is not Prakṛiti as such, but Prakṛiti evolved into manas. In mukti it is manas which, having achieved all its purposes, changes form by way of being resolved into the form of its cause.

Holding one or another of these views as to what happens in mukti the yogin of the Sânkhya school stoutly opposes the doctrine of the followers of the Upanishads as to the manas becoming one with A'tman, on the ground that manas could be resolved only into Prakriti, its cause. Afraid on these and similar grounds and held captive by avidyâ, they reject the doctrine of amanîbhâva established beyond doubt by both S'ruti and the experience of the sages, and regard it as mere sushupti. These yogins regard themselves very wise, though altogether devoid of true wisdom. They practise restraint of breath and do other hard things with a view to realise the true A'tman. But as the blind can never see the treasure though held in the palm, never can such men reach the fearless Blissful Self though ever present in their own hearts.

The doctrine of Vaiseshikas and Madhyamikas.

Though self-luminous as the witness of every act of thought, and always free from all upâdhis, still some philosophers, such as Vaiśeshikas, and Mâdhyamikas, hold that A'tman is naturally devoid of consciousness. The Vais'eshikas* hold that A'tman has, in himself, neither consciousness nor bliss, and that he becomes conscious only when in contact with manas; while the Mâdhyamikas† hold that A'tman

* The followers of Kanâda.

† The nihilistic school of Buddhistic metaphysicians.

never possesses them. Both of them are labouring under a delusion, and declare that *amanastâ* or freedom from the sway of manas is possible only at the time of moksha or at death, not during life.

Higher Grade of Yogins.

The best class of aspirants comprises those who look upon manas, the sense-organs and all the rest as a mere fiction apart from Brahman's being, just as, where a rope is mistaken for a serpent, the serpent is a mere imagination. They are themselves Brahman, and in virtue of the very wisdom which they have acquired; fearlessness and the endless Peace—the manifest unsurpassed Bliss—called moksha exists in their very being and does not depend on anything else. These men of wisdom are Jîvanmuktas, having already attained to mukti. Hence no need for them to tread the path any more.

Lower Grade of Yogins.

Others again—all those yogins who, doing righteous deeds and thus treading on the right path, have purified their buddhi, but who hold to beliefs removed one or more degrees from the absolute truth,—are convinced of the independent existence of manas, which is held to be quite distinct from Átman and yet in contact with Átman. To them who have not attained to the conviction that A'tman alone is real, fearlessness—*i. e.*, sâkshâtkâra or direct perception of A'tman, the Supreme Reality—is unattainable except by the restraint of manas. With reference to this class of aspirants, the âchârya says :

"Dependent upon the restraint of manas is fearlessness for all yogins; as also extinction of pain, and true wisdom, and also endless peace." (verse 40).

For him who does not distinguish A'tman from non-A'tman extinction of pain can be brought about only by the restraint of manas; for, pain must necessarily arise so long as manas, which is always in contact with A'tman, is subject to motion. Moreover, that insight also into A'tman which has already been spoken of as fearlessness depends altogether on the restraint of manas. Similarly, that endless Peace which is called moksha is dependent on the restraint of manas.

Inferior Yogins should practise mental restraint.

Accordingly all yogins should resort to the restraining of manas in the manner recommended by those who are versed in the traditional knowledge of the process. We say '*all* yogins' advisedly, inasmuch as even the hitherto misguided yogins will ultimately reach the goal if they would but turn away from their former course and begin to work in the right path. He who desires the well-being of his own Self (A'tman) should first conquer manas; and the conquest of manas, though hard to achieve, must be possible, because S'âstra enjoins it and the sages have borne testimony to its being a fact of their own experience.

Strong will and cheerfulness are necessary.

The aspirant should practise restraint of manas with a resolute and cheerful heart:

"Like the emptying of the ocean by the tip of kus'a grass, drop by drop, so has the restraint of manas to be achieved without weariness." (verse 41.)

Those who exert themselves strenuously, never dispirited in their antaḥ-karana,—that is, never chafing thus: "when the eye is closed, I see darkness; when I open my eyes I see objects, such as a cloth or a pot; never am I able to see Brahman;"—whose first resolution to conquer manas is perhaps like the resolve to dry up the ocean by pouring out its water drop by drop with the tip of a kuśa grass; never wearied or despondent, they can achieve the restraint of manas.

The legend of tittibhas.

The legend about the attempt to empty the ocean by pouring out its water drop by drop is narrated by tradition as follows :—

Once upon a time there lived a couple of *tittibhas* on the shore of an ocean beaten hard by surfs. The male bird, puffed up with pride, set the Ocean at naught and left the newly laid eggs on the shore, despite the remonstrations of the wife. He then addressed her thus : " Do not fear, my dear! If the Ocean be so proud as to carry off my eggs, then I shall deprive the infatuated fellow of all his water ; and you will then see him quite powerless by fear." The wife shewed him in many ways what an impossibility it was. What was he when compared with the Ocean ? The husband, however, left the eggs in the same spot and went with the wife in search of food.

When they were gone, the Ocean who had all the while been listening to the conversation, with all his pride carried off the eggs by his big surfs. But remembering the Supreme Lord, the Ocean thought thus within himself : " All things, animate and inanimate, are the manifestations of the Supreme Lord. There is no knowing what may happen to a being, when, by whom, or how. His Mâyâ works miracles in the world. I am not sure who he (the tittibha) is, what his abode, who his friends, what his power or his time. I shall therefore keep his eggs safe in a place." Thus thinking, the Ocean secured them in a safe place and roared aloud as before.

When with a full belly the *tittibha* returned to the place with his wife, the eggs were missing. He was beside himself with anger and resolved to dry up the Ocean. Then his well-meaning wife addressed him thus : " What are you, a small creature born of an egg, compared with the mighty

Ocean? Why do you wage war against him, against all reason? Alliance or enmity is fitting only among equals. You and the Ocean are not equals. Thy body is but sixteen inches long, and thy wings not more than a foot wide. Thy legs are like the stem of a mango-fruit, and thy beak is like the kuśa grass. Thy wings are soft like silken cloth and no more than twelve inches. So small is thy whole extent, either within or without. Time is ever the same with one born in the brute creation. Time produces change in mankind, in Devas and Daityas." Friends you have none except myself, a poor and helpless creature. Enemies become friends in consideration of the money to be got in future or of the good reception at the hands of the wealthy. But even that wealth dost thou of the feathered creation lack. Thou canst not fly in the air even to the distance of an arrow's flight. By birth thou art *tittibha*, the meanest of the oviparous race. Whereas, the Ocean is a million miles long on one side and two million miles on the other, and he is as deep as the earth itself." At the time of cosmic pralaya he floods all the three worlds by his waves as a lake inundates the earth by its outlet." He holds within him quite as many beings as there are on earth; and in him there are precious gems of all sorts. Among his friends may be reckoned powerful Devas and Munis of great austerity," and he holds for the Devas and men an inexhaustible supply of gems." He has given refuge to the mighty mountains such as Mainâka when they were afraid of Indra Thus do thou think all about thyself and the Ocean. Do not in vain provoke enmity leading to thy death. Already by thy folly I have lost my children. Do not by thy death add to my misery." "

When thus harangued at length, his eyes became red and his hair stood on end. With a firm resolve he addressed his wife, who looked quite miserable, as follows:

" In times of prosperity friends are found in millions, but he who is a friend in need is a friend indeed. Whoso forsaketh in need is an enemy, even if it be the son or the wife. He is a friend, who is a firm adherent in virtue and sin, in happiness and misery. But as an enemy is he to be regarded who, trusted as the very self for his wisdom, proudly prattles much in adversity. He who seeks success in life should slay first the enemy who is disguised as a friend, and then the declared foe. So, though a friend in appearance, thou speakest like a foe. But I think it is wrong to slay one of the weaker sex, and I abstain therefore from the sin. As the wise say, seven paces make friendship. I have lived long and happily with thee ; how shall I now injure thee, a friend and a woman ? So, do leave this place and go elsewhere. Do not tarry here. Alone, by my own might, I will dry up the Ocean. With my beak and my two wings I will pour out his water and ere long reduce him to a shallow pool."

Thus saying, he flew into the air and began to work, with a view to dry up the ocean. The hen-tittibha saw his resolve, and as a dutiful wife begged his pardon and followed suit. Both day and night, without being tired, they worked to dry up the ocean. They dipped their beaks and wings to pour the water out ; but the water evaporated so soon as was taken up. They, however, went on doing so for a long time, when other tittibhas began to dissuade them from the attempt. They were merely told to evince their friendship by co-operating with them in the attempt to dry up the Ocean or else to go back their way. Thereupon they joined the couple in the act of pouring out the water ; and so did the rest of the feathered race of all classes. Then, at last, Nârada, the Divine sage, wending on his unimpeded course through the three regions, saw these birds at work and tried in many ways to dissuade them. But they did not desist.

Seeing they were firm in their resolve, he advised them to invoke Garuda's help. At the very sight of the fierce Garuda the ocean trembled with fear and restored the eggs to the tittibhas."

Thus untired like the *tittibhas* should a person work at the subjugation of manas. Once he makes a firm resolve, Gods will come to his help in the same way that Garuda came to the help of the tittibhas. Help invariably comes from all beings in a righteous act. Even the monkeys helped Râma to recover his wife. He can achieve all, who possesses the attributes of manliness, self-control, courage, strength, skill and prowess. No man should ever abandon an undertaking, great or small, just as the lion never retraces his steps when once he has begun to march. Bearing all this in mind, he who engages in the subjugation of manas should never turn back even in the face of a deadly foe.

Obstacles to Samadhi.

It should not, however, be supposed that unwearied effort alone can help far in the subjugation of manas. If that were an adequate means of conquering manas, then there would be no necessity for the other ways pointed out by the scriptures. On the other hand, there are various obstacles in the way of the man who practises samâdhi with a view to attain to sâkshâtkâra, to an intuitive realization of truth. They are enumerated as follows: *laya* (mental inactivity), *vikshepa* (distraction), *kashâya* (passion), and *sukharâga* (taste for pleasure). So, manas should be restrained from falling into these states, by resorting to the ways recommended below. Otherwise the object of the practice cannot be attained.

The neophyte should study the scriptures, and then reflect and meditate upon them. By this course, supplemented by his unwearied efforts to restrain manas, he can acquire a knowledge of the True.

S'rî-Gaudapâdâcharya teaches us what those snares are and how to avoid them or how to escape from them:

Vikshepa and laya.

" By skill should one restrain manas when distracted by kâma and enjoyment, and even when it is tranquil in laya. As kâma is, so is laya." (Verse 42).

When manas becomes distracted by desires and objects of desire, the neophyte should restrain it by resorting to the course described below and cause it to dwell on A'tman. Moreover, he should restrain manas from getting into laya or mental inactivity—which is equivalent to the sushupti state,—though it be a state which is marked by the absence of all trouble. Laya or mental inactivity is as much a source of evil as kâma, and therefore it is that manas should be prevented from lapsing into that condition as much as it should be restrained from kâma.

Antidotes to vikshepa and laya.

The A'chârya points out the means of avoiding or escaping from vikshepa and laya:

"Ever thinking that all is pain, he should restrain (manas) from the enjoyment of Kâma; ever thinking that all is the Unborn, he never sees the born." (Verse 43).

"In laya let him wake up the chitta; when distracted, let him withdraw it again. Let him know it is (then) *sakashâya* (impassioned); when balanced, let him not disturb it." (Verse 44).

By always thinking that all duality set up by avidyâ is only a source of pain, he should withdraw the wandering manas from objects of enjoyment to which it has been led by kâma. This is the means known as *vairâgya-bhâvanâ*,—practice of dispassion or indifference to worldly pleasures by thinking of their impermanence and evil nature. By always meditating on the instructions of the śâstra and the Teacher, which point to the doctrine that the Unborn or Brahman is all—that is, by what is called *jñânâbhyâsa*, by a repeated study, reflection and contemplation of the teaching of the śâstra,—he never sees the born, the world of duality as opposed to Brahman, because it does not exist.

Thus by the twofold means of jnânâbhyâsa and vairâgya-bhâvanâ, let the neophyte wake up manas sunk in laya, in nidrâ or sushupti ; *i. e.*, let the manas be engaged in seeing A'tman as distinguished from non-A'tman. When distracted by desires and pleasures, let him at once withdraw the mind from them.

Kashaya and its antidote.

Though, by repeated practice, manas is awakened from laya and its wandering checked by the twofold process of jnânâbhyâsa and vairâgya-bhâvanâ, still it is far from having attained perfect balance, the state of the unconditioned Brahman. When in this intermediate stage, the manas is known to be *sakashâya* or impassioned, as still possessed of *râga* or attachment which is the seed of all its activity in the direction of external objects. From this state, as from the states of laya and vikshepa, manas should be restrained by a special effort, by means of what is known as *Samprajñâta-Samâdhi*,* and brought to a perfectly balanced condition, *i. e.*, to the state of *Asamprajñâta-samâdhi.**

---

* Samâdhi is of two kinds, (1) *Samprajñâta* or *Savikalpaka*, and (2) *Asamprajñâta* or *Nirvikalpaka*. When manas is engaged in profound contemplation of Brahman, always thinking "I am Brahman," at a certain stage it

When once by the twofold Samâdhi manas tends to a state of perfect balance, to that of the unconditioned Being, it should no longer be disturbed; care should be taken that it does not again fly towards sense-objects.

Rasasvada and its antidote.

There is yet another obstacle which the A'chârya treats of in the following verse:

"Let him not taste the pleasure therein. Without attachment let him resort to wisdom. Let him with effort make the steady chitta one when it tends to go out." (Verse 45).

The Yogin who wishes to attain to Samâdhi should not taste the pleasure which manifests itself in the Samâdhi state: he should restrain manas from cherishing any longing even for the intense pleasure which is felt in *Savikalpaka-Samâdhi*. What should he do then?—Without longing for the pleasure, he should have recourse to discrimination: *i.e.*, he should dwell on the thought that the pleasure which is found to

---

assumes the form of Brahman, but without ceasing to think of a distinction between the meditator and Brahman who is meditated upon. So long as this distinction continues in thought, the samâdhi is said to be in the *savikalpaka* or *samprajñâta* stage. When this distinction disappears in thought altogether, when manas is *en rapport* with Brahman so as to be completely identified with Him, it is said to have reached the *asamprajñâta* or *nirvikalpaka* stage of samâdhi.

arise in the Savikalpaka-Samâdhi is a mere fiction due to avidyâ and is therefore false, and that whatever is accidental is a mere fiction like the serpent imagined in a rope. Thus, the yogin should prevent the mind from longing for even this sort of pleasure. When again manas, though restrained from a longing for the pleasure by vairâgya and made to dwell steadily in the Átman by practice of Samâdhi, still tries to assert its nature and is inclined to wander outside by a longing for pleasure and objects of pleasure, it should again be restrained with effort from so wandering, by resorting to the means already described, such as jñânâbhyâsa and vairâgya. To sum up: by practice of Samprajñâta-Samâdhi culminating in Asamprajñâta-Samâdhi, the aspirant should make manas one with Para-Brahman and he himself should remain as the pure all-full Brahman.

Manas identical with Brahman.

When does manas become completely identical with Brahman? The Áchârya says:

"When the chitta is not dissolved nor is distracted again, unmoving and unmanifesting, then it becomes Brahman." (Verse 46).

When, thus freed from all obstacles and completely withdrawn from sense-objects by jñânâbhyâsa and other means described above, manas is no longer subject to laya nor resolved into its cause nor distracted by external objects, and is steady like the lamp-flame in a windless spot, not manifesting itself as an external object of any kind,—then manas has become Brahman.

Brahman realized in Nirodha-Samadhi.

Brahman as realized when manas attains to a state of perfect balance—*i.e.*, to what is called Asamprajñâta-Samâdhi—is described by the Áchârya as follows:

"Existing in itself, tranquil, endued with bliss, indescribable, it is the highest bliss; unborn, as the Unborn-Knowable; they declare (it) Omniscient." (Verse 47).

Thus, manas in Asamprajñâta-Samâdhi is the very Brahman, is the Real Bliss, the Reality of the Self. It exists by itself, by its own greatness, *i.e.*, it is quite independent of all. It is Peace, the cessation of all evil. It has attained to Nirvâna. It is indescribable and quite an uncommon thing. It is the highest bliss felt by yogins only. The Brahmavids declare that this bliss and knowledge is unborn, unlike sensuous pleasure and knowledge, and as such it is one with the Unborn, with That which we seek to realize. Being omniscient it is identical with the omniscient Brahman who is bliss itself.

The farthest limit of the process of restraint.

How long is this process of restraining to be carried on? The S'ruti says:

4½. So long only should it be restrained, till it attains dissolution in the heart.

When manas is dissolved in the heart-lotus, all external perceptions being replaced by the consciousness "I am Brahman," then there is no more need for restraint; and it has been shewn, by quoting the sayings of Teachers belonging to the line of the Ancient Tradition, that the dissolution of manas consists in attaining to a state of perfect equilibrium, *i.e.*, to the state of Brahman.

Restraint of manas is the essence of all worship.

How then is it that no jñâna or dhyâna is taught here? It is only restraint of manas that is taught here. But mere restraint cannot constitute a human end.

In reply the śruti says:

5. This is jñâna and dhyâna; the rest, mere dispute and prolixity.

This restraint of manas constitutes *jñâna* the *sâkshât-kâra*, an intuitive perception of the fact that 'I am Brahman'. It is this restraint which conduces to jñâna. The jñâna which results from an investigation of the śâstras ultimately takes the form of this nirodha. Yoga, too, is the same. It constitutes also dhyâna, the meditation that 'I am Brahman.' In short, nirodha is the culmination of sânkhya and yoga, and it is the nirodha which underlies all other sâdhanas or spiritual exercises. All else, all acts other than the restraining of manas within, are tantamount to quarrels of disputants. He who constantly studies śâstras may acquire erudition, the main result being no better than mere waste of breath. Any more teaching in books forms a mere string of words. So, a wise man should content himself with a moderate amount of book-learning. All except what contributes to the restraint of manas and to a knowledge of its process, does not in the least lead to real happiness. Charity, worship, austerity, purificatory ablutions, pilgrimages to sacred places, vedas and learning,—all this is useless to a man whose manas is not tranquil. Therefore, above all, one should practise restraint of manas. By restraint of manas one can achieve all his aspirations, here and hereafter. Without it no human end that is good can be attained.

Highest end attained by restraint of manas.

It has been said that when manas has been completely restrained, the highest end of man is attained. How?

6. Never to be thought nor unthought, unthinkable but altogether worthy of thought is That, free from one-sidedness; Brahman, then, it becomes.

This highest stage now attained cannot be thought of as an external something which is agreeable to the mind. Neither has it to be avoided in thought, as an external object of dislike. It cannot be spoken of by any word of mouth; and while immersed in this samsâra, none can think of it. It can only be thought of as the immortal Self. It cannot even be felt as any sensual pleasure can be. Nevertheless it is none other than the eternal unsurpassable self-luminous bliss which is quite worth contemplating. It is the very thing described as the True, Intelligent and Infinite Bliss and so on. In the nirodha state when manas is free from all activity, it becomes Brahman, the same in all beings. When manas is free from all predilections caused by friendship or enmity, then man becomes Brahman without much ado.

Perfect restraint of manas possible.

Or the verse may be explained as an answer to the question, how can manas ever attain to an unthinking state, to the condition of Brahman, inasmuch as there always is something to be constantly thought of and something else to be constantly avoided in thought?

6. The unthinkable has not to be thought of; nor is what is thinkable to be avoided in thought; then freed from all one-sidedness it becomes Brahman.

The Reality being quite inaccessible to thought, there is really nothing to think of. Neither is there any necessity for forgetting anything; for, the external objects of sense which alone the mind can ever think of, have no real existence. When thus freed from one-sidedness—from the thinking of the Real and the forgetting of the unreal,—then manas becomes Brahman.

Restraint of manas by means of Pranava.

The śruti proceeds to point out the way in which the restraint is to be effected :

7. By sound let a man effect Yoga. Then let him meditate upon the not-sound. Then by the realization of the not-sound, the non-being is seen as being.

By meditating upon Pranava—upon its constituent sounds—in accordance with the instructions of the śruti and the Teacher, the aspirant should achieve Yoga, the restraint of manas, culminating in the knowledge 'I am Brahman.' When firmly established in Pranava, he should meditate upon the Pranava beyond sound, *i.e.*, he should dwell on the mere idea without the help of the sound. When meditation without the help of the sound reaches the culminating point in the form of the intuitive knowledge 'I am Brahman,' then, in the absence of avidyâ and all its effects, is seen the essence of Brahman free from all limitations. There remains then nothing but Brahman, who is Existence, Intelligence and Bliss in essence.

Or, the meditation here enjoined may be described as follows:

By svaras, by the vowels *a* and *u*, *i.e.*, in the jâgrat-svapna* state which these vowels represent, yoga should be practised. By earnestness and zeal, the practice of yoga is possible even in the jâgrat-svapna state. He should then meditate upon *m* which is next to the vowels *a* and *u* in *Om*, *i.e.*, upon the ânanda state which is next to jágrat-svapna. Thus meditating on *m* or ânanda state, one attains, not to the non-being, but to the all-full Being, the Turîya or the Fourth state. So it is elsewhere said, "By *m* beyond the vowels, one reaches the subtle state."

---

* *Jâgrat-svapna* is defined to be that state of manas in which—whether restrained by yoga or not—it returns to itself and is exclusively concerned with its own subjective world, never going out towards external objects of sense.

Manas completely restrained is Brahman.

In the nirodha state manas is not reduced to a nullity. It is the particular form of this or that object assumed by manas which distinguishes it from Brahman. But when manas is engaged in the thought of the unconditioned Átman, then the pure Brahman's being as existence in the abstract divested of all forms becomes manifest. The real nature of a thing does not merely consist in the particular form in which it presents itself to the senses ; it exists also as existence in the abstract. That which manifests itself in manas when all its particular forms are neutralized is none else than Brahman. Accordingly the S'ruti describes this state of being thus :

8. That verily is partless Brahman, which is beyond all thought, unstained. Knowing " That Brahman am I" one becomes Brahman, the immutable.

That *be-ness* which manifests itself when avidyâ and the rest are absent is Brahman. It is devoid of all phases of manifestation such as prâna.* It transcends all. It cannot be described as this or as *not* this. It is unstained by avidyâ

* The other kalâs or phases of being are : faith, ether, air, light, water, earth, sense, mind, food, vigour, penance, hymns, sacrifice, the worlds, and name. (Praśna-Upanishad, v. 4).

which is the seed of all evil. Brahman of this nature is intuitively realized by all Brahmavâdins. To them the Self which is self-luminous consciousness and bliss and which is present in the mind of every one as his Ego is not different from Brahman, the Infinite. Thus perceiving intuitively his identity with Brahman, the yogin becomes the very Brahman.

Brahman known to the wise only.

It is known only to the enlightened ; for It is

9. Beyond all thought and Infinite, beyond argument and illustration, unknowable and causeless; knowing which, the wise man is liberated.

It is not limited by space and time, nor is it limited by other things. Nothing can be inferred about It. In short It is accessible to no instrument of cognition. But there is the wise man who, having realised Brahman, has been liberated. He is quite familiar with Brahman as described above. When the Átman is known and manas has undergone dissolution, to the manas-less yogin Brahman thus described becomes self-manifest.

Atman ever changeless.

Now the following question may arise: if it be admitted that manas is subject to birth and death and that the Átman who is unattached and indifferent to all is really affected by the attributes of manas, then the Átman must be possessed of those attributes.

The śruti says in reply :

10. No death, no birth; not the bound, nor the aspiring; not the seeker of liberation, nor the liberated: this is the supreme truth.

There is really neither manas nor the body subject to birth and death; none really bound by the bonds of avidyâ etc.; none practising sannyâsa, brahmacharya and the like subsidiary acts. There is really none who seeks moksha. What appears to be the birth and death of manas, the renunciation of this or that man, all this is false, not real. This notion is an intuitive conviction of consciousness, and is the real truth.

Atman beyond the three states.

Question :—The Átman passes through jâgrat, svapna and sushupti states. As no being can pass through these three conditions without undergoing change, how can there be no death etc. ?

In answer, the śruti says :

11. In jâgrat, svapna and sushupti, it should be thought that there is one Átman alone. To Him who has risen beyond the three states, there is no longer any birth.

It should be understood that the Átman, the self-luminous witness of Buddhi, present to every body's consciousness as the Ego, is one alone, undergoing no change in all the three states of consciousness—namely, *jâgrat*, the state of sensuous perception of objects ; *svapna*, the state in which the mind is conscious of the impressions left upon itself by previous sense-perception ; and *sushupti*, the state in which the mind is unconscious of any particular object. He is the *Turiya*, the Fourth ; He is beyond the three states. He is unaffected by the birth etc. of the three states. Once a man realises 'I am Brahman' he is no longer subject to birth anywhere, at any time, or in any manner, though by illusion he has hitherto fancied that he was subject to it.

Atman appears different owing to upadhis.

It may be asked, how can one appear as many ? In answer the śruti says :

12. For, one only is the Self in all beings, appearing different in different beings. As one, and also as many, is He seen, like the moon in water.

The Átman is one only in all beings, moving and unmoving ; there is none else of the same or different sort. Nor is there any division into parts in the Átman. The one Átman appears different in different beings, putting on the form of the bodies and the antah-karanas in which He manifests Himself.

Though He is one in virtue of His essential nature as existence, intelligence and bliss, He appears as many in the many upâdhis. He appears as one when the upâdhi is one, and as many when the upâdhis are many. To illustrate: in a vast expanse of water there is only one image of the moon reflected; and when water is contained in many vessels, the reflected images are as many. This illustration is intended to show that the jîva is to be conceived as a reflection of the I'śvara, whether we hold that there is only one jîva or that there are many jîvas. But the illustration is more apt when the jîva is supposed to be one only. Once the full meaning of this scriptural statement is clearly understood after being taught by the Guru, the enlightened man, in whatever state he may be,—in the jâgrat or svapna or sushupti state,—should ever meditate that the Átman who is beyond the three states is one and the same in all persons. He who knows the Átman who is beyond the three states shall even become the Átman. On learning that the Átman is free from all the differences, the idea of plurality associated with jîva will disappear by reflection and reasoning.

Analogy of Atman to akasa.

Here follows a description of the real nature of Paramátman:

13. Just as, when a jar is carried (from place to place, it is) the jar (that) is carried

(from place to place), not the âkâśa—the âkâśa which is enclosed as it were in the jar,—so, jîva is like the âkâśa.

This is intended to illustrate the view that jîva is I'śvara with an upâdhi. When, on death, the body passes from one region to another, the Átman who is enclosed as it were in the body goes nowhere. It is the body alone that passes from one region to another.

How Atman differs from akasa.

Jîva is not like the âkâśa in all respects:

14. Like the jar, (the body) is of different forms, breaking up again and again. And (âkâśa) knows not that it is broken, while He always knows.

The jar breaks up again and again, but never the all-pervading âkâśa; so, too, the body etc. undergo decay again and again, but not the Omnipresent Átman. The illustration applies only thus far. As regards consciousness there is a difference. When the jar is carried from one place to another or when it is broken, the âkâśa does not know it; whereas the jîva, the self-conscious blissful Átman, is ever conscious of the changes the body etc. undergo.

How jiva is identical with Brahman.

Jîva is one or many. If jîva is one only, it cannot be different from Átman, each of them being one, and of the same nature as the other. A'tman is thus described in the śruti:

"He is the one God, hidden in all beings, all-pervading, the Self within all beings, watching over all works, dwelling in all beings, the witness, the perceiver, the only one, free from qualities." (S'vetâśvatara-Upanishad, VI, 11).

If there be many jîvas, even then jîva cannot be different from A'tman. A'tman being the essence of jîva, jîva cannot be conceived to exist apart from A'tman. Although A'tman is identical with jîvas who are many, there can be no plurality in A'tman, who is all-pervading. A'tman is one in the many jîvas, as the genus is one in the many individuals which make up the genus. In point of fact, there is not even one jîva distinct from A'tman. How can there be many? What apparent differences there are among jîvas are only due to the differences which are found in the upâdhis with which the A'tman is connected. If, out of these upâdhis, be eliminated that element of reality which pertains to the basic substance, the A'tman, then the upâdhis themselves become unreal.

This identity can be seen from the illustration cited above of the jar and the âkâśa. A'tman without the upâdhis—the physical (sthûla), subtle (sûkshma) and causal (kârana) bodies—corresponds to the mahâkâśa or the vast expanse of âkâśa; while jîva in the body corresponds to the âkâśa of the jar.

Except through the upâdhi of the jar, the âkâśa in the jar cannot be distinguished in any way from the mahâkâśa.

Relation between Atman and jiva.

This illustration of âkâśa and jar serves to indicate many other facts concerning the relation between jîva and Átman:

(1) When the idea of limitations caused by a jar etc. is removed from the mind, the limited âkâśas become merged in the mahâkâśa; so also when jîvas are distinguished from their upâdhis, they become one with Átman. This points to the fact that liberation is coeval with knowledge.

(2) When the âkâśa enclosed in one jar is associated with dust and smoke, the other limited âkâśas are unaffected by the dust and the smoke; so, too, when one jîva is associated with pleasure or pain, other jîvas are unaffected by it. For, pleasure or pain pertains only to the upâdhi, which is not the same in all jîvas.

(3) The âkâśas in the jar etc. have different names given to them, serve different purposes, and assume different forms according to the upâdhis, while the âkâśa in itself remains unchanged. So, too, different jîvas are associated with different forms and names and serve different purposes according to the upâdhis, while the Átman remains one and the same in them all.

(4) The âkâśa in the jars etc. cannot be said to be a part or transformation of the mahâkâśa; so jîva can never be a part or modified form of A'tman.

(5) Just as to children the âkâśa appears as if stained with dirt, so, also, to the unenlightened manas A'tman appears as bound, as tainted with sin.

(6) When a thing comes into existence or is destroyed, when a body goes or comes, the âkâśa within undergoes no change; so also the A'tman. Accordingly, no jîva, be it one with A'tman or different, is ever born or ever dies; for, birth and death pertain only to the body. It is, therefore, meaningless to say that the jîva is born and dies. Just as jîvas, as seen in dreams or projected by the juggler's art (mâyâ or indrajâla) or imagined to dwell in an artificial idol, are supposed to be born and to die though actually no jîvas are born and die in them; so, too, all these jîvas are devoid of birth and death, and it is only by illusion that they are said to be born and to die. Thus no birth or any other change ever befalls jîva. On the other hand, it is only the chitta or manas undergoing these changes that cause them to appear to pertain to the A'tman. It is only when the jîvas come in contact with manas and identify themselves with manas that they appear to be born &c., though immutable in themselves.

Unreality of phenomena.

In point of fact even manas has no real existence. Really it is identical with Chit, the Absolute Consciousness. Manas is consciousness in motion, as it were. This aspect of manas is described by Gaudapâdâchârya, the mouthpiece of ancient tradition, in his kârikâs on Mândûkyopanishad, *Alâta-śânti-Prakarana* (verses 47—52). He speaks of manas as consciousness in motion. Manas in motion being consciousness in motion, manas at rest being identical with Absolute Consciousness.

" It is the firebrand* in motion that appears straight, crooked and so on. So, too, it is the consciousness in motion that appears as perceiver and perception." (Verse 47).

Consciousness only *appears* to be in motion owing to avidyâ. There can be no motion in consciousness which is immutable. Absolute Consciousness is partless, all-pervading, unborn and immutable. This mere semblance of motion in consciousness which all the while undergoes no real change is what is called *vivarta* or illusory change.

" The unmoving firebrand produces no such phenomenon and is unborn† ; so, too, consciousness without motion produces no phenomenon and is unborn." (Verse 48).

---

* The glowing end only is meant here.

† *i. e.*, as straight or crooked.

The same firebrand, when at rest, does not appear as straight or crooked. So, too, consciousness which was in motion as it were owing to avidyâ ceases, on the cessation of avidyâ, to move and give rise to phenomena.

For the following reason also we should regard the phenomena as false:—

"When the firebrand is in motion, the phenomena do not come from without. They are not gone elsewhere when it is not in motion, nor do they enter the firebrand." (Verse 49).

We have not seen these phenomena coming from without into the firebrand when it is in motion, or going out of the firebrand when it is at rest. Nor do they enter into firebrand when it is at rest; for it is not their *upâdâna* or material cause. If firebrand were to be regarded as the material cause and motion as the efficient cause of the phenomena, then on the withdrawal of the latter cause, *viz.*, motion, the effect should still reside in the material cause; for it cannot be proved that mere absence of the efficient cause is accompanied by disappearance of the effect*. Thus the origin as well as the disappearance of the phenomena being quite inexplicable, the phenomena themselves must be false.

* In the case of a pot, clay is said to be the material cause, and the potter etc. the efficient cause. Once a pot is produced, it will not necessarily disappear on the withdrawal of the efficient cause.

"They do not go out of the firebrand, because they are no substances; and so also in the case of consciousness, inasmuch as they are equally phenomenal." (Verse 50.)

The phenomena of straightness and crookedness are no real substances. They cannot, therefore, be said to go out of the firebrand as from a house. Indeed it is a real substance that can enter or go out of another substance. So, too, the phenomena of birth and death associated with consciousness are no realities, because they are mere appearances like the straightness and crookedness of the firebrand in motion.

When consciousness is in motion, the phenomena do not come from without. They do not go elsewhere out of the consciousness when it is at rest, nor do they enter consciousness. They do not go out of consciousness because they are not substances, unthinkable as they always are, being unrelated as cause and effect"

(Verses 51—52.)

It cannot be held that, consciousness being somehow in motion, these phenomena of birth etc. come into it from without; for, there is no testimony of consciousness to that effect. Nor can it be held that, consciousness being immutable, these phenomena have their being elsewhere; there being no testimony of consciousness to this effect either. Neither can it be said that when they disappear these phenomena enter into consciousness; for, it can never be held that consciousness by itself is the upâdâna or material cause. Moreover, being unsubstantial and unreal, they cannot enter into or go out of consciousness.

Then it may be asked, how is it that they present themselves to consciousness?

We answer: they are illusory. It being impossible to suppose that consciousness and these phenomena are related to each other as cause and effect, the phenomena are ever inexplicable, and as such they are mere illusions and are therefore unreal.

Thus, consciousness is like the firebrand in all respects, only consciousness is never really subject to motion,—it is always immutable. Not being related as the effects of any cause, as things produced out of something else, the phenomena are non-entities and are therefore undefinable. In the case of the firebrand appearing as straight or crooked, there exists really nothing straight or crooked, and yet there arises with regard to the firebrand the consciousness of a straight or crooked thing; accordingly, though birth etc. do not really exist, the idea of birth etc. arising with reference to pure consciousness is an illusion.

Maya and its action.

A mere word sometimes gives rise to an idea without the corresponding reality, as for instance, "a man has a horn." Mâyâ or illusion produces the same effect, as when a juggler causes the phenomenon of a city in the air. So, the idea of this whole world of duality arises by word and by mâyâ. In fact everything else besides Átman is unreal.

Even this word and this mâyâ are not real. Existing as it does only by the name 'mâyâ', mâyâ is not real. There is no evidence to prove that mâyâ has a real existence. The word, too, is unreal, existing only in name. But unlike them, Átman is inaccessible to thought or speech and does not therefore depend on them for existence. Átman is *svayamprakâśa* or self-conscious, shines by Himself and is independent of all.

A question now arises: Why, if Átman is omniscient, is He not always aware that He is essentially the Bliss (ânanda) itself? The answer follows:

15. Veiled by word-illusion, never goes one by darkness to the Holy Place. And darkness removed, the One alone sees the Unity.

Mâyâ (illusion) is a mere word, having no corresponding reality. It is a power capable of achieving impossibilities and is the cause of the whole universe we perceive around us by the senses, of the universe comprising both subtle and gross objects of nature. It looks very fine when not closely examined. He who is veiled by this mâyâ is deprived of the knowledge that he is the very Bliss (ânanda) in essence. He sees himself a limited being, though he is really identical with the infinite Brahman; just as a pot when immersed deep in water looks very much smaller than it actually is. On account of this darkness, of ajñâna caused by word-illusion, one does not recognise one's own holy blissful Átman that pervades all; like a man, who, though having eyes and knowing all, cannot at all, when surrounded by thick darkness, reach a holy place or thing situated ever so near. When this darkness of ajñâna is pierced through by the light of wisdom realising the unity of the Real Ego with Brahman, then immediately all distinctions such as perceiver and perceived being absent, the jîva stands alone as the self-luminous Átman and sees his identity with Brahman.

Yoga for the realisation of the Unity.

Now the śruti proceeds to describe the yoga by which to realize this unity :—

16. The syllable Om, the Word, is Para-Brahman. That disappearing, he who knows That which is the Indestructible should meditate upon that Indestructible, if he would seek peace for himself.

First the word, the syllable 'Om,' should be meditated upon as Parabrahman. The three mâtrâs or the component parts of 'Om,'—*viz.*, *a*, *u*, *m*,—

respectively denote the three upâdhis of Parabrahman, *viz*., the sthûla (gross), the sûkshma (subtle) and the kârana (causal) aspects of cosmos. When these three aspects of cosmos, together with the three mâtrâs of the Pranava representing them, gradually disappear, there remains the One alone which is beyond the three upâdhis, hence called the *Turíya*, the Fourth. It is indestructible, and as transcending all differentiations it is the Unity above referred to. Therefore he who wishes to realise this Unity, the Supreme Brahman, should first practise the meditation of Brahman as identical with Pranava or some such word. Then knowing this Unity,—this Indestructible Blissful A'tman—as treated of in the sâstra, the wise man should continuously meditate upon It as one with himself, if he would at all attain moksha, the cessation of all pain caused by avidyâ and other sources of evil —leading him to identify himself with the body as though it were himself or something belonging to him.

Lower and Higher Wisdom.

17. Two vidyâs, verily, need to be known, the S'abda-Brahman and what is known as the Supreme. The adept in the S'abda-Brahman reaches the Supreme Brahman.

Both sorts of wisdom, what we call and know of as vidyâs, are necessary for a mumukshu to acquire.

One of them is what is known as S'abda-Brahman, that lore which comprises the vedas including the syllable *om*, *vyâhṛitis** (the utterances), *angas* (auxiliary sciences), and *upavedas* (minor vedas); the other being the Para-Brahman described as the Real Existence, Intelligence, Bliss and so on.

It is no doubt true that inasmuch as a knowledge of Parabrahman leads to the consummation of happiness, it is necessary to know Parabrahman. The other lore, however, is not altogether useless. He who has thoroughly mastered the drift of the teaching of the S'abda-Brahman, of the vedas etc., can soon know "I am Para-Brahman".

On attaining the higher, the lower should be given up.

On knowing the Para-Brahman, the S'abda-Brahman should be given up:

18. Having studied books, the wise man, solely devoted to knowledge and wisdom, should give up the books entirely, like the man who, seeking for rice, gives up the husk.

After making the S'abda-Brahman his own by a study of the texts comprised therein together with their meaning, the student who can keep the teaching of these texts in mind without forgetting should devote himself to knowledge and wisdom (jñâna

* They are seven: Bhûh, Bhuvah, Suvah, Mahah, Janah, Tapah, Satyam.

and vijñâna).—Jñâna and vijñâna may be thus distinguished from each other: one of them consists in the sâkshâtkâra or the direct perception that "I am Brahman" from which all idea of dhyâtṛi and dhyâna, of meditator and meditation, are absent; while the other consists in the knowledge that "I am Brahman" as taught by the S'âstra, involving all such distinctions as meditator and meditation on the part of the student.

Unity of Vedic wisdom.

19. Of the cows of different colours, the milk is of one colour only. The wise man regards wisdom like unto milk, but its forms like unto the cows.

Though the cows may each be of a different colour, white, black, red, &c., their milk is of one colour only, namely, white. So, too, knowledge taught by all the Vedas is the same, though there are different texts taught by different teachers and known by different names, such as S'ânkhâyana Kaushîtaki, Mâdhyandina, Katha, Kanva, Taittirîya and so on.

The latter part of the verse is also explained thus: The A'tman is the same in different bodies which are found to behave differently in different, individuals. In all beings there is only one Átman who can be known only by manas exalted by study, reflection and contemplation.

The latter part of the verse is explained in yet another way: The wise man culls wisdom from Vedas after careful investigation, just as cowherds take the milk of cows after careful examination.

Meditation necessary.

For this purpose, manas should be brought under control and made to dwell on the Átman the subject of our search:

20. Quite concealed in all beings dwells Vijñâna as butter in milk; ever churn, O aspirant! with manas as the churning stick.

The Vijñâna, the Átman who is Consciousness and Bliss, lies hidden in the body. Do thou, O aspirant, always meditate upon the Átman.—In this figurative representation, curd represents all beings; the churning stick, manas; the churning rope, the notion that 'I am Brahman'; and butter, the Átman, the secondless. The extraction of butter represents moksha, the extrication of the soul from the ocean of samsâra.

21. With the churning rope of knowledge one should rouse up the Supreme, like unto the fire. "Partless, motionless, tranquil, such a Brahman am I"; so it has been found.

Churning produces fire also.* Hence the second illustration, "like unto the fire." Fire here no

* Sacrificial fire is produced by churning. Vide verse 11.

doubt stands for sâkshâtkâra which elsewhere is spoken of as fire: "The fire of wisdom reduces, O Arjuna, all actions to ashes" (Bhagavad-Gîtâ, iv. 37). Or Agni may stand for Pranava: one should repeat Pranava.

The first part has also been explained as follows: with the eye of the knowledge that "am Brahman" —free from all doubts andmisconceptions—do thou unearth the Supreme, as gold from a mine. This idea of identity of the Self with Brahman is the organ by which to see Brahman, to attain the sâkshâtkâra that "I am Brahman."

"I am Va'sudeva."

Brahman and Átman have been thus shewn to be identical. The śruti now concludes this proposition, the main drift of the S'âstra, only speaking of Brahman as Vâsudeva.

22. Of all beings the abode; He who, as gracious to all, dwells in all beings; He am I, Vâsudeva.

Vâsudeva: He is *vâsu* because, by His grace, He dwells in all beings, and all beings dwell in Him; and He is *Deva* because He is self-luminous, shining by His own light.

II.

KAIVALYA-UPANISHAD

WITH

COMMENTS.

KAIVALYA-UPANISHAD.

FIRST KHANDA.

Introduction.

This upanishad is so-called because it teaches the means by which the soul can completely emancipate itself from matter and further transmigrations. Nârâyana* calls this upanishad, especially the first of its two sections, by the name of S'atarudrîya, *i. e.*, literally, a century of designations applicable to Rudra. To distinguish it perhaps from the so-called S'atarudrîya, namely, the fifth prapâthaka of the fourth kânda of the Taittirîya-Samhitâ, beginning with '*Namaste rudra manyave,*' he call this upanishad *Brahma-Śatarudrîya*, *i. e.*, that S'atarudrîya which is dedicated to the glorification of the Nirguna or Unconditioned Brahman, as opposed to Saguna or conditioned Brahman, the personal God called S'iva, who is glorified in the other. According to Nârâyana it is this Brahma-S'atarudrîya which is recommended for recitation in the second khanda.

* Nârâyana-tîrtha and S'ankarânanda have written comments on this and many other Upanishads.

S'ankarânanda, S'rîkantha-S'ivâchârya* and others, however, speak of only one S'atarudrîya, *viz.*, that which occurs in the Taittirîya-Samhitâ.

Brahmavidya.

1. Then did A's'valâyana approach the Lord Parameshthin, and said:

Do thou, O Lord! teach Brahmavidyâ, the most excellent, always resorted to by the righteous, quite hidden, by which the wise man ere long shakes off all sin and reaches the Purusha (Spirit), greater than the great.

Then: after the acquisition of the four qualifications (sâdhanas), *viz.*:

(1) *Viveka*: discrimination between the real and unreal.

(2) *Vairâgya*: indifference to enjoyments here and hereafter.

(3) 1. *S'ama*: control of manas.

2. *Dama*: subjugation of the senses.

3. *Uparati*: abstention from all formal religious rites, accompanied with the renunciation of all desires.

---

* He has written a commentary on the Brahma-Sûtras interpreting them so as to mean that S'iva is the Supreme Brahman.

4. *Titikshâ* : endurance.

5. *Samâdhâna* : ability to fix manas on one single object for a long time.

6. *S'raddhâ* : faith in the teachings of the Veda and of the Teacher.

(4) *Mumukshutva* : a longing for liberation.

A's'valâyana : the son of A'śvala, a teacher of Rig-Veda. *Parameshthin* : (lit. dwelling in the Supreme Abode), Brahmâ, the father of all, known also as the Pitàmaha or Grandfather. Áśvalâyana approached Brahmâ in due fashion and put him a question with a view to learn Brahma-vidyâ, the Divine Wisdom. *Brahma-vidyâ* : that knowledge which leads to an intuitive perception of Brahman, the One, Infinite in time and space. This Brahma-vidyâ exists in the hearts of all beings; only it is quite concealed from view by avidyâ. It is resorted to by those who have subjugated the body and the senses, and it is well guarded from those who are not qualified for it. *The wise man* : he who has realized that his own true Self is Brahman. *All sin* : all cause of pain which may be summed up in ajñâna and its vâsanâs or latent impressions. *Greater*, &c. : Avyakta which is the cause of the whole universe is great, and the Átman, the Supreme Lord, who is the seat and object of the highest wisdom, is even greater than Avyakta. He is called Purusha because He is all-pervading.

Threefold Path.

2. And to him, verily, He, the Grandsire, said : do thou know it by means of Faith, Devotion, and Meditation. Not by work, not by progeny, nor by wealth, but by renouncement, the Great Ones attained immortality.

The Grandsire: Brahmâ the "Lotus-seated" is the father of Daksha and other Prajâpatis who are the fathers of the whole universe. Because Brahma-vidyâ cannot be directly said by word of mouth,—Brahman transcending all speech and thought,—the Teacher proceeds first to teach the means by which it can be attained. There are three means of attaining Brahma-vidyâ : (1) *S'raddhâ* : the firm faith that there is something beyond the visible and that what the Scriptures and the Teachers teach concerning the Invisible is nothing but truth. (2) *Bhakti* : complete devotion to the Guru and to the Lord who is the Goal of the Path. (3) *Dhyâna* : deep meditation, an unbroken current of the thought of Âtman, uninterrupted by any other thought. Endued with S'raddhâ and Bhakti, the aspirant attains Brahma-vidyá by practice of meditation. Like S'raddhâ and Bhakti, Sannyâsa—the renouncing of all sacrificial rites and everything dear in the world —constitutes a means of attaining Brahma-vidyâ. By renunciation alone the great sages acquired the ancient wisdom and attained immortality. Without renunciation, no intuitive or direct knowledge of A'tman can be attained. Without renunciation, it is at best only an indirect knowledge of the Reality that can be attained.

When the aspirants resort to complete renunciation,

The Goal of the Path.

3. That which is higher than svarga, That which, seated in the cave, shines resplendent,—That do those aspirants enter, who by vedântic wisdom have well ascertained the Thing,—those aspirants whose minds have been purified by sannyâsa-yoga.

4. In the regions of Brahmâ, at the last moment of Para, they all become released from the Great, the Immortal.

The aspirants of unsullied minds,—those who, having renounced the world, by mighty effort attained an intuitive realization of Brahman,—become, while still alive on earth, one with their own immortal blissful A'tman far transcending svarga.

If by any obstacle, such as a desire to enjoy the pleasures of Brahmaloka, those aspirants who, after renouncingall world as something not worth longing for, have ascertained the nature of Brahman by the study of the scriptures, fail to attain in their earthly life to a complete realization of their identity with Brahman, they go after death to the regions of Brahmâ the Demiurge, and there they as well as Brahmâ will be completely liberated at the last moment of Para, the great cycle of Brahmâ's life, *i.e.*, at the time of Pralaya or Kosmic Dissolution,—not before,—and become one with the Absolute Brahman.

Contemplation of the Nirguna-Brahman.

The S'ruti now proceeds to describe the Yoga by which He who dwells in the heart of all may manifest Himself to the disciple in his own heart.

4½. At a retired spot, seated in an easy posture, pure, erect being the neck, the head and the body ;

5. Leading the highest order of life, restraining all the sense-organs, and having saluted his own Guru in devotion, regarding the heart-lotus unstained and quite pure, and in its centre contemplating Him who is free from all taint and grief ;

6. Who is Unthinkable, the Unmanifest, whose forms are endless; who is the Good, tranquil, immortal ; who is the womb of Brahmâ ; and who is devoid of a beginning, middle, or end ; the One ; who is Intelligence and Bliss ; the Formless ; the Wonderful.

For the attainment of Brahman, the aspirant should practise yoga in the following manner. He should resort to a clean and lonely place, and when there is nothing to disturb the mind he should sit on a comfortable seat. He should then perform all the internal and external ablutions prescribed by the S'âstras, without any feeling of trouble. Firmly seated in a regular posture—such as Padmâsana—he should hold erect his head, neck and body. He should become a sannyâsin of the highest or Paramahamsa order. Restraining the mind and all the senses, he should bow down to his own Guru with Bhakti as laid down by law, regarding Him equal to Devas, if not even superior to them. He should then regard the heart-lotus as perfectly pure, free from all râjasic and tâmasic dirt, free from all passions and delusions, etc.,—containing within it the orbs of the sun, the moon and the fire. Within it he should contemplate the Parameśvara, the Unmanifested and the Unthinkable, as transcending all speech and thought; the Infinite; the Good; the Bliss itself; free from Mâyâ, free from birth and death, the One, self-luminous, endued with all powers; the source of all Vedas; the Formless; quite a wonderful Being.

Contemplation of the Saguna-Brahman.

If the mind cannot rise to think of Parameśvara as such, he should contemplate Him in His Saguna or conditioned aspect as made up of the Lord and His Spouse.

7. Him whose help-mate is Umâ ; who is the Supreme Lord, Mighty, Three-eyed; Dark-necked, and Serene : having meditated thus, the sage reaches Him who is the womb of all beings, the witness of all, transcending darkness.

Umâ : S'iva's help-mate, *i.e.*, the Brahma-vidyâ which protects Śiva from such assailants as passion, love, etc. Or, Umâ may refer to the Goddess Bhavâni associated with Śiva, the Lord, conceived as half man and half woman. The aspirant should contemplate Umâ,—the Divine Lady spoken of in the Kena-Upanishad as an incarnation of Brahma-vidyâ,—as a help-mate of the Supreme Lord conceived as man. This Divine Lady is the prototype of all other beings of the female sex, who may be looked upon as Her mere reflections. She is the Divine Being composed of all potencies (Śaktis) and all principles (Tattvas). It is by Her Grace that all living creatures including Devas attain to svarga or moksha in future, and to worldly happiness on earth. By Her mere glance, Brahmâ, Vishnu, Rudra, S'akra and other Devas exist or cease to exist. Possessed of a high and broad chest, wide loins, slender waist, moon-like face, fish-like eyes, black hair, the Divine Lady, beautiful in every limb of the body, cannot but bewitch the heart of Her Divine Lord. Bedecked with a jewelled belt in her waist, with bracelets in the wrists, arms and ankles, with garlands of pearls and other jewels round the neck, with an ornamental crown and earrings, and with many other jewels, she shines with incomparable splendour. Though the mother of the whole world, yet she never looks more than sixteen years old.

Associated with such a Divine Lady is He, the Divine spouse, even more perfect in all attributes, the Overlord of Brahmâ and other mighty beings, bedecked with all sorts of ornaments. Clad in the tiger's skin or quite naked, His whole body is smeared with ashes. He wears a garland containing a number of Brâhman-skulls, with a digit of the moon shining in His clotted hair. Brilliantly white like cow's milk, He wears the Ganges on the head and puts on a smiling face. He is a thousand times more beautiful than Kandarpa, the god of love, and a thousand times more brilliant than the sun. Himself without birth and death, He is the cause of the birth, existence and dissolution of the universe. His face is as handsome as the full-moon, and He has the sun, the moon, and the fire for His eyes. Every part of the body is very beautiful, His neck being shaped like a conch. He has arms extending down to the knees and wears a serpent as the sacred thread (yajñopavita) the over body. He is seated in Padmâsana, with the eyes resting on the tip of the nose. He is called *Mahâdeva* and *Vâmadeva*, the highest and the most gracious God. He is the first Guru of all Gurus. He is self-luminous. He is Bliss in essence. He is without a second. From Him was born the Hiranyagarbha, the father of the Virâj and of all the other Devas.

The aspirant whose mind is not equal to the contemplation of the Nirguna-Brahman, the Absolute, should resort to Yoga and contemplate the Parameśvara as described above; as Dark-necked, as the Lord of the universe, as the destroyer of all sins, as seated in the heart-lotus, or in the sun, or in the fire, or in the moon, or in the Kailâsa or some other mountain. When the manas of the Yogin who contemplates the Divine Being in this form as half-man and half-woman becomes steadfast, then he realizes S'iva—that wonderful Supreme Divine Being, who is the cause of the universe and yet who is devoid of the whole or any part of the universe, who transcends all speech and thought—as his own true Self who is above all delusion and never tainted by it, who is a mere witness in the Buddhi of all beings while in himself unconnected with it.

Brahman is all.

He whose helpmate is Umâ and who is reached by the meditation described above, has no.

avidyâ. To the enlightened, He is the Self of all, He is all. When the Lord is conceived as associated with Umâ, He is said to be the Saguna or conditioned Brahman. That same Lord is the Nirguna or unconditioned Brahman; for, when all avidyâ has vanished, none else will be found to exist besides the Lord, who is all.

8. He is Brahmâ, He is S'iva, He is Indra, He the Indestructible, the Supreme, the Self-luminous; He Himself is Vishnu. He is Prâna. He is Time, He is Fire, He the Moon.

9. He Himself is all, what has been and what is yet to be, the Eternal.

He is Brahmâ, Vishnu, Rudra, S'akra and all other Gods; He is fire, the sun, the moon and Time; the eleven senses, the antah-karana in its four aspects, the five prânas, the five mahâ-bhûtas, the main and intermediate quarters, the up and down, all beings of life, the Brahmânda (Brahmâ's Egg or the Mundane Egg) itself which is the body of the Virâj, the Virâj himself, the Hiranyagarbha, Jîva and I'śvara, Mâyâ and its modifications, the manifest and the unmanifest; what was and what is yet to be;—all these are the Maheśvara and none else. Just as one man alone becomes many in dream, so the one Deity exists as many. Just as the city of the Gandharvas appears in the sky where there is really no such city, so all this manifold material existence proceeds from, appears, endures and ultimately dissolves in the single Bliss-A'tman.

Knowledge of Brahman is the sole path to liberation.

Except by a realization of the one secondless A'tman, except by realizing beyond all doubt that the One Self is in all beings and all beings are in the One Self, there is no other way for liberation,—there never was in the past, nor will ever be in the future. Accordingly the śruti says:

9½. Having known Him, one crosses beyond death. There exists no other path to liberation.

10. Seeing the A'tman abiding in all beings and all beings in the A'tman, one reaches the Supreme Brahman,—not by any other means.

Meditation by Pranava.

When the meditation practised on the line recommended above does not lead to the right knowledge of Brahman, then the neophyte should have recourse to the meditation of the One Self by means of Pranava:

11. Having made the A'tman the *arani*, and Pranava the upper *arani*, by practice of knowledge, by repeated churning, the wise man burns up the bond (pâs'a).

Two pieces of wood (of the śamî tree, respectively

termed *uttara-arani* and *adhara-arani*, the upper and lower aranis) are used for kindling sacrificial fire by attrition, one being placed above the other. These two pieces of wood are rubbed together by churning with a stick which has a string running round it. The practice of meditation is compared to the process of churning fire for sacrificial purposes. One's own body,—the aggregate of all the sheaths of the Self,—corresponds to the lower *arani*; the three-syllabled *Om* to the upper one; manas to the churning stick; the repeated act of meditating to the act of churning; and what is called the A'nanda-Átman or the Bliss-Self to the fire produced by churning. That is to say, by a constant reflection and meditation—by means of Pranava—of the thought "I am Brahman, the Self of all," the non-dual Self manifests itself in the heart of the yogin. Once this fire of the non-dual Self is brought into existence, the yogin will be able to burn up all ajñâna and kâma, which are known by the name of Pâśa (bond), giving rise to the ties of 'I' and 'mine'. When these are burnt up, the Self will remain alone by Himself.

A'tman in jagrat, svapna and sushupti.

It may be asked, whence comes the bond of samsâra to him who is secondless and who, free from attachment, is indifferent to all? In reply the śruti says:

12. It is He who becomes deluded as to the real Self by Mâyâ, and who, seated in the body, does everything. He it is who, while awake, attains satisfaction by women, food, drink and other divers pleasures.

13. In svapna, He, the jîva, is the enjoyer of pleasures and pains in all world created by his own Mâyâ. At the time of sushupti, everything vanished, by darkness (tamas) enveloped, He attains the blessed condition. And again, in virtue of Karma of past births, the self-same jîva dreams or becomes awake.

The jîva who burns up all bonds by Self-knowledge,—by the knowledge that his real Self is Brahman,—becomes identical with Brahman. In himself he is without attachment and quite indifferent to all. When completely veiled by His own Mâyâ, Brahman is called Purusha or Jîva. Veiled by Mâyâ which has the power both of concealing the true nature of the Self—which is self-luminous and blissful,—and of causing engrossment in things external to the Self, he lives in the body composed of various sheaths, gross and subtle, identifying himself with it. Thus he does many an act and reaps the fruits of his own acts.

In the jâgrat state when external objects are perceived by organs of sensation, he puts on various bodies, and enjoys pleasures or suffers pains of various sorts caused by the external objects ; though all the while it is not the Real Self that enjoys or suffers.

When in *svapna* or dream all the organs of sensation are quiescent, the jîva enjoys and suffers in a world of his own composed of things—such as cars, horses, elephants—which are all the creation of mâyâ, of ignorance and misconception, inasmuch as they are nothing but the re-vivified impressions which have been left on the manas in the jâgrat or waking state. In jâgrat, as much as in svapna, the jîva perceives objects which are mere creations of mâyâ.

When in sleep he is unconscious of external objects and all consciousness of the external world is merged in its cause (ajñâna), then it is that the jîva enjoys his own inherent bliss, but without being aware of it. Thus, the same Self that has been associated with the jàgrat and svapna states now passes into sushupti ; and then he is free from vikshepa ; he is completely shut out from all external world. He then enjoys his own inherent bliss ; but, being then overpowered by Tamas, he (rather his manas) is not conscious of the fact.

Maya is the cause of Atman's samsara.

In samsâra, as in the jâgrat and svapna states, we enjoy or suffer in a world of mâyâ. By mâyâ the Self becomes variously deluded and is merged in samsâra. Just as under the influence of certain drugs and incantations a man loses all knowledge of himself, so under the influence of mâyâ he knows nothing of the Self. While thus causing in jîva forgetfulness of the Self, mâyâ gives rise to a further delusion. It makes him think that he is a samsârin. This is merely due to his association with mâyâ. When found associated with thieves, even an innocent man is regarded a thief and punished. There is in reality no mâyâ in jîva. Mâyâ itself is a creation of mâyâ. In âkâs'a, for example, where there is no form or colour, the unenlightened man sees form and colour. Though undeluded in himself, the A'tman becomes deluded while in samsâra, like a man who, however educated and wise while awake, sees all sorts of unrealities in his dreams. So long as the sleep of mâyâ continues, there is no end of misery for jîva.

Guru is the Deliverer.

The jîva who has been sorely suffering from the throes of samsâra is at length awakened by a merciful and gracious Guru. Thus enlightened, he no longer sees any misery at all. The jîva acquires this enlightenment only as the result of a vast store of good karma he has done in the past. This state of enlightenment is called the fourth state; and it is a condition to which very few can attain.

Jiva is identical with Brahman.

The A'tman, who as jîva causes the synthesis of the whole body and life, is identical with Brahman.

14. And it is verily from Him, who as the jîva amuses himself in the three bodies, that the whole variegated being is born. He is the basis, the Bliss, the Infinite Wisdom, in whom the three bodies and (all) get dissolved.

15. From Him are born prâna, manas, and all the indriyas; the âkâs'a, vâyu, light, water, the earth which maintains the whole universe.

The gross body, the subtle body and ajñâna constitute the three bodies which are the scenes of jîva's enjoyment. These three bodies become extinct only when the jîva has entered into the fourth state, but not otherwise. So long as jîva is ignorant of his true Self, he puts on body after body according to his karma, and abandons each when it is worn out and no longer fit for enjoyment. So long as avidyâ continues, he is born again and again: he is now a child, then a youth, then a decrepit old man, and then he dies; then again he is born and passes through all the stages, and so on. Thus by avidyâ he oscillates unceasingly in samsarâ like the pendulum of a clock. When jîva attains to the fourth condition, he becomes that Being, the Absolute Brahman, who is said to be the basis of all existence. He is the self-luminous Bliss itself. He brings the whole universe into being out of Himself, there being no material causes nor instruments external to Himself. From Him who is the Lord of the three bodies and the Witness in Buddhi, is born prâna and manas; that is, He is the source of all activity and knowledge, of Kriyâs'akti and Jñânas'akti: from Him are born all senses, organs, &c.

The Grand Truth.

It is this fourth condition which the great Gurus, the Mahâtmans, teach as the true being of the Self to such of their disciples as have purified their hearts of all dirt. This is what the Vedântins call the Mahâvâkya, the Grand Utterance, whose teaching, declaring the unity of Brahman and Jîva, is expounded in this Upanishad as follows:

16. That Supreme Brahman, the Self of all, the great abode of the universe, subtler than the subtle, the Eternal, That is thyself, and thou art That.

Brahman: the Infinite, unlimited by space. *The Self of all*: dwelling in the hearts of all beings and one with them all. *Thou art That*: though an enjoyer and doer by avidyâ, thou art in reality none other than the Supreme Brahman.

Realization of Truth leads to liberation.

The śruti now declares what the fruit is of a knowledge of this truth:

17. That which illumines the universe composed of jâgrat, svapna, sushupti and so on,—knowing "I am That Brahman", from all bonds one is released.

I: the knower of Brahman, the self-conscious Bliss, the Self. *Bonds*: of egoism.

Atman is not identical with the Universe.

Átman is of a different nature from the whole universe, as the s'ruti says:

18. Whatever in the three states is the object of enjoyment, the enjoyer and the enjoyment itself, from them distinct am I, the Witness, the pure Intelligence, the Ever-Good.

Three states: jâgrat, svapna and sushupti. *The Ever-Good*: Sadâśiva, or Mahâdeva who is the Pure, Eternal Good itself.

The Disciple's recognition of the True Self.

When thus taught by the gracious Guru, the disciple recognizes his True Self and thus declares his experience:

19. In me all is born, in me all things firmly stand, in me all attains dissolution. So, I am Brahman, the secondless.

In me all is born, etc: I being none other than Brahman.

Immutability of Atman.

One should not suppose that because Átman is thus the cause of the world's origin, stay and dissolution, He is of the same form as the world and changes with it. On the other hand, Átman is never subject to change : His nature is inscrutable and very hard to realize. The s'ruti says :

20. I am verily subtler than the subtle, so am I the Great ; I am the universe diverse ; I am the ancient, I am full (Purusha), the Ruler, I am the Golden ; and the Auspicious am I in form.

The Golden : full of wisdom ; that Self in the Sun who underlies all the things in universe.

Atman is Omniscient.

Though Átman has no hands and other organs of action or of sensation, He is omniscient. So the S'ruti declares :

21. Without hands and feet I am of unthinkable activity ; without eyes, I see ; without ears, I hear ; distinct (from Buddhi), I understand ; and there is none who knows Me ; I am ever conscious. I am He who is knowable by the many Vedas : I am the Maker of the Vedânta, as well as the Knower of the Vedas.

I am the Holy One, the Great Omniscient Lord,

without duality, inaccessible to all speech and thought. *I am the Maker of the Vedânta* : I am the Revealer of the truths taught in the upanishads; I am the Teacher of all sciences; I am the God beyond the universe.

Atman is formless.

As the śâstra declares, Átman is devoid of all form:

22. To me there is no virtue or sin, no death or birth, no body, senses or buddhi. No earth or water exists for me, and no fire, and no air exists for me, nor ether.

The whole universe is made up of mâyâ and the rudimental elements (bhûtas); these and the things made of them are only illusory appearances of the self-conscious Bliss, of Átman who is altogether free from duality.

The Sakshatkara.

The immediate result of an intuitive recognition of the identity of the Self with Brahman is described by the Śruti as follows:

23. Thus knowing the essence of the Paramâtman, the Supreme Self lying in the cave, partless and secondless, the Witness of all, having neither the existent nor non-existent,—one reaches the pure essence of Paramâtman.

Lying in the cave: dwelling in the Buddhi of all as the witness of all its functions.

SECOND KHANDA.

Recitation of the Satarudriya.

In this section the s'ruti proceeds to teach how to purify the antah-karana which, owing to its impurity, is unable to comprehend the Supreme Self:

1. He who recites the S'atarudrîya becomes purified by sacred fires; he has atoned for wine-drinking; he has atoned for brâhmanicide; he has atoned for voluntary and involuntary sins. Thereby he is refuged in the Avimukta, (the Lord). He who is of the highest order should recite it always, or once.

2. By this he attains wisdom which is destructive of the ocean of samsâra. Therefore, having thus known Him, he attains liberation as the result.

Avimukta: He who is distinct from the jîva, from the *vimukta* or the abandoned. *Avimukta* is one of the names applied to the sacred place now called Benares. It is so named because it is *never*—not even at the time of pralaya—*deserted* by S'iva and S'akti, by the I'śvara and His Prakriti, who dwell there in perfect bliss. The place itself is full of Divine Bliss, as the abode of the Blissful Divine Pair, and it is said to have been created from the Divine Feet as the region where the Divinity may abide when the whole universe is merged in dissolution. This sanctuary is identified by the Yogins with the region of the human body between the chin and the forehead,—with the nasal root where the two eyebrows meet. It is, by pre-eminence, the seat of jîva inasmuch as when Manas is concentrated there, the individual consciousness reaches the lower levels of I'śvara who, enrobed in the Supreme Light of Divine Consciousness (Para-Chit), wards off and destroys all sin brought on by sensuality. In whatever part of the world he may live, the Yogin whose thoughts dwell on the Divinity manifested in this region called A'jñâ-Chakra—the region where a *slight glimpse* into the Divinity is attained—lives in the real sanctuary called *Kâśî* (the shining one), *Avimukta* (the undeserted), *A'nandakânana* (the forest, or manifestation, of Bliss), *Vârânâsî* (that which wards off and destroys all sins), *Rudrâvâsa* (Rudra's abode), Mahâśmaśâna (the great cremation-ground). *The highest order*: the order of Sannyâsins known as Paramahamsas.

When, owing to an impure manas, a man is not equal to the contemplation of the Nirguna-Brahman or even of the Saguna-Brahman, then he should not resort to *nyâsa*, *i. e.*, the fourth sacerdotal order of

Sannyâsa. On the other hand he should constantly recite the holy chapter of the Veda, called Rudrâdhyâya, which washes away all sins. There is no text in the whole Veda superior to it. By the recitation thereof his heart becomes pure and attains extreme vairâgya or indifference to worldly objects. Vairâgya indicates that chitta, the thinking principle, has become pure. Then he may enter on the fourth order. Even then he should continue to recite the Rudrâdhyâya and contemplate S'iva as Uma's Spouse, till he attains the Sâkshâtkâra or direct cognition of the Supreme Self. While thus engaged in the recitation, he should at the same time pursue the study of the Vedânta, always endued with strong faith and rendering service to the Teacher. He who perseveres in this path will soon attain spiritual illumination.

ERRATA.

p. 71. l. 13, *for call* read calls.

p. 75. ll. 7-8 should be in small print.